EFFECTIVE
COMMITTEE
SERVICE

SURVIVAL SKILLS FOR SCHOLARS

Managing Editor: Mitchell Allen

Survival Skills for Scholars provides you, the professor or advanced graduate student working in a college or university setting, with practical suggestions for making the most of your academic career. These brief, readable guides will help you with skills that you are required to master as a college professor but may have never been taught in graduate school. Using hands-on, jargon-free advice and examples, forms, lists, and suggestions for additional resources, experts on different aspects of academic life give invaluable tips on managing the day-to-day tasks of academia—effectively and efficiently.

Volumes in This Series

1. **Improving Your Classroom Teaching**
   by Maryellen Weimer

2. **How to Work With the Media**
   by James Alan Fox & Jack Levin

3. **Developing a Consulting Practice**
   by Robert O. Metzger

4. **Tips for Improving Testing and Grading**
   by John C. Ory & Katherine E. Ryan

5. **Coping With Faculty Stress**
   by Walter H. Gmelch

6. **Confronting Diversity Issues on Campus**
   by Benjamin P. Bowser, Gale S. Auletta, & Terry Jones

7. **Effective Committee Service**
   by Neil J. Smelser

8. **Getting Tenure**
   by Marcia Lynn Whicker, Jennie Jacobs Kronenfeld, & Ruth Ann Strickland

9. **Improving Writing Skills: Memos, Letters, Reports, and Proposals**
   by Arthur Asa Berger

10. **Getting Your Book Published**
    by Christine S. Smedley, Mitchell Allen & Associates

SURVIVAL SKILLS FOR SCHOLARS

EFFECTIVE COMMITTEE SERVICE

NEIL J. SMELSER

SAGE Publications
International Educational and Professional Publisher
Newbury Park   London   New Delhi

Copyright © 1993 by Sage Publications, Inc.

For information address:

 SAGE Publications, Inc.
2455 Teller Road
Newbury Park, California 91320

SAGE Publications Ltd.
6 Bonhill Street
London EC2A 4PU
United Kingdom

SAGE Publications India Pvt. Ltd.
M-32 Market
Greater Kailash I
New Delhi 110 048 India

Printed in the United States of America

Library of Congress Cataloging-in-Publication Data

Smelser, Neil J.
 Effective committee service / Neil J. Smelser.
    p.   cm. — (Survival skills for scholars ; vol. 7)
 Includes bibliographical references.
 ISBN 0-8039-4818-2. — ISBN 0-8039-4819-0 (pbk.)
 1. Meetings—Handbooks, manuals, etc. 2. Committees—Handbooks,
manuals, etc. 3. Congresses and conventions—Handbooks, manuals,
etc. I. Title. II. Series.
AS6.S564 1993
658.4'56—dc20   93-8616
                                                     CIP
 93 94 95 96   10 9 8 7 6 5 4 3 2 1

Sage Production Editor: Yvonne Könneker

Contents

Preface   vii

Acknowledgments   xii

1. **The Committee as Creature**   1
   One Name, Many Functions   2
   A Jumble of Committee Types   10

2. **Giving Birth to Committees**   16
   Forming a Committee   16
   Charging the Committee   23
   Staffing the Committee: The Art of the Possible   32
   *Staffing Committees: Why Do People
   (and Why Should You) Serve?*   39

3. **Inside the Black Box**   43
   The Instrumental Side of Committee Life   44
   The Expressive Side of Committee Life   49
   The Evolution of a Committee Culture   57

4. **How to Serve**   60
   Knowing Your Assignment   61
   Knowing When You Are Being Co-opted   62
   Knowing How to Represent Your Constituencies   63
   Timing Your Interventions   64

Keeping Your Comments in Context   65
Following Through on Your Contributions   66
Not Attacking Other Committee Members   66
Relying on Humor   67
Avoiding Extremes and Self-Scapegoating   68

5. **How to Chair**   **70**
Knowing Your Assignment's Limits and Demands   72
Knowing the Committee's Purpose   73
Knowing What Resources to Expect   74
Knowing the Committee's Size and Composition   75
Negotiating Before Accepting the Chair   75
Responding Directly to the Collective Task   76
Keeping the Business Moving Without Hurrying   76
Openness and Accommodation   79
Dealing Directly With Conflict   79
Staying on Top of Terminal Tensions   81

6. **The Committee Report**   **82**
The Structure of the Report   82
Strategies for Writing Committee Reports   85

7. **Committees and Careers**   **98**

   Appendix   **103**

   About the Author   **108**

Preface

This book emanates from the experience of a veteran server on committees. It is intended both as an analysis of those organizational creatures and as a guidebook for those of you who have served, do serve, and will serve on committees—which probably includes all of you.

I begin with a vital item of advice. When serving on a committee, you should never let yourself become 100% involved in its business. If you do, you will surely be driven to distraction by the sheer mass of inefficiency, irrelevance, and tedium that committee meetings entail. You must leave ample room for relief from this dreaded effect through some other kind of mental activity—silently reviewing the heroics of yesterday's ball game, for example, or simply daydreaming during someone else's useless speechmaking.

To preserve my own sanity, over the years I have developed the habit of doodling on Styrofoam cups with multicolored ballpoint pens during committee meetings. I have worked this up into a kind of elaborated folk art, producing symmetrical designs of modest aesthetic value. For the benefit of those of you with an artistic turn of mind, Figure 1 reproduces one of these cups. At the end of a given meeting, I typically present such a cup as gift to the fellow committee member who shows the greatest—or even the slightest—interest in or admiration for my artwork.

Figure 1. Doodled-on Sytrofoam Cup

Recently, however, my habit has been threatened by a national move against Styrofoam, fostered by our increasing ecological consciousness. The city of Berkeley, for example, which is very environmentally aware, frowns on Styrofoam. Faced with this adverse public opinion, I now drive across the Berkeley-Oakland border late at night, buy Styrofoam cups at an Oakland supermarket, and bring them back home like so much contraband. If the pressure against Styrofoam continues to grow, I may have to give up committee work altogether.

No organization runs without committees. If we scan the landscape of contemporary organizational life, we find them to be omnipresent creatures. Academic organizations are no exception. In fact, they are probably honeycombed with more committees than their counterparts in other institutional spheres—business firms, hospitals, civil service bureaucracies, and military units, for example. There is a good reason for this. The main currency of colleges and universities is collegial influence, not the exercise of power and authority. It might even be said that if an order has to be issued in academia, that is a sure sign of organizational failure. Committees, moreover, are generators and peddlers of influence. They gather information, reflect, make recommendations, and advise—in short, they influence—as academic organizations move through their eternal cycles of routine functioning, problem solving, crisis meeting, and decision making.

One does not have to be a card-carrying functional analyst to observe that, being omnipresent, committees serve a great variety of both manifest and latent functions in academic and other organizations. I will review some of these functions in Chapter 1. At the same time, our feelings about the committee often resemble our feelings about a spouse in a neurotic marriage: We need and are dependent on it and may even love it sometimes, but we also detest it and wish in vain that we could shake free from it. This ambivalence is reflected in familiar bits of cynical humor.

Forming a committee is thought to be a substitute for decisive action: "When in doubt, form a committee." Committee work is felt to be a boring and useless chore. Committees engage in "make work." And committees are believed to produce vague, wishy-washy, lowest-common-denominator results: "A camel is a horse drawn by a committee." Yet, as in a neurotic marriage, we keep falling back and relying on the committee as a tried and true organizational mechanism.

Every one of us in academia has served on some kind of committee or committeelike group. Even when a department chair asks a couple of colleagues to sit down, think about an issue or problem, and come up with some ideas, an informal committee is at work. In my own academic career, which is now approaching four decades, I sometimes feel as though I have served on every committee in and around academia. That is false, of course, but there have been very many. I have served on committees of my department, my campus academic senate, my campus administration, my multicampus academic senate, my multicampus university administration, other universities, professional associations, foundations, boards of trustees, and the U.S. government. "Smelser reports" emanating from these assignments litter the filing cabinets and wastebaskets of dozens of bureaucracies. The Appendix lists as many of these committees as I can remember. All the examples in this little book come from my committee experiences through the years, but in the interest of maximizing expository continuity and avoiding scattered illustrations, I will focus on a selected few.

In serving on all of these committees, I have run the gamut of the ambivalent feelings noted above. Sometimes committee work has been engaging, even exhilarating. At other times it has been boring. To counteract the latter effect, I have developed another defense—in addition to cup doodling—against the less enthralling aspects of committee work. I have assumed a kind of dispassionate, anthropological distance and have studied the committee as a creature. The reflections I have developed in doing this are the contents of this book. I hope my observations ring true and prove helpful. Even if they do not, I hope they may provoke a modest raising of consciousness about this important aspect of our professional lives.

As indicated, this book contains both analysis of and advice about committee work. In offering the latter, I do not intend to suggest that all of you should behave as I have behaved on committees. Everyone develops his or her own style in groups, and many different styles can be effective. Nevertheless, some rules of thumb can be articulated, and I present these as general guidelines, always with the caution that you should read them as such and not as eternal principles.

The book is organized by a logic that corresponds in part with the life course of committees. As indicated, Chapter 1 is an orienting chapter, revealing what kind of creature a committee is; what it does in, for, and against the organizations in which it is embedded; and specifying the major kinds of committees. Chapter 2 deals with the birth of committees: how they should be formed, charged, and staffed. Chapter 3 concentrates on how committees work, how they develop conflicts, and how they forge a distinctive committee "culture." How to serve on committees is the topic of Chapter 4, how to chair them that of Chapter 5. Chapter 6 deals with the strategies of writing a committee report. To wrap things up, Chapter 7 offers broad observations and advice about the place of committee service in an academic career.

Acknowledgments

I should like to thank Mitch Allen of Sage Publications, Inc., for urging me to write this book and for his helpful substantive and editorial advice throughout. I knew there was such a book in me, and he provided the right opportunity for its realization. Christine Egan, my longtime assistant, also deserves thanks for processing the whole project very efficiently. The actual pages were written during my 1-month residency at the Bellagio Study and Conference Center in May 1992. That splendid setting on Lake Como was the perfect one for such a project, and I record my appreciation to the Rockefeller Foundation for supporting me.

1 | The Committee as Creature

A committee never has an existence in and of itself. It is always embedded in a larger organization or is a part of a larger political process. If this context is not understood, those who work on committees lack direction, and they operate even more in the organizational dark than they normally do. There are no hard and fast rules for dealing with a committee's organizational environment, but there are features about it that can be understood. In this chapter I attempt modestly to increase that understanding.

To that end I pose two simple but essential questions:

1. What do committees do for and against organizations—or, alternatively, what are their functions?
2. What are the major types of committees?

The two questions are related to one another, because function often affects form and structure, and vice versa (see Box 1.1). Furthermore, you must know about both the functions and types of committees if you are to anticipate correctly what they demand of you and what kind of experience you will have while working with and on them.

Box 1.1

The Many Functional Faces of the Committee

The committee as:
- Collective thinker
- Umpire
- Unifier
- Rubber stamp
- Competitor in the power game
- ... and probably more

One Name, Many Functions

In this section, I present not only obvious and manifest functions, but also subtle and latent functions.

The Committee as Collective Thinker

Every committee has a mission to improve organizational rationality and the quality of organizational functioning. It accomplishes this, moreover, by gathering information, reflecting on that information, entertaining alternative lines of action, and either rendering a decision or advising decision makers on the basis of this process. Several examples come to mind:

- Many university campuses have a standing committee called a *committee on courses*. It is composed of faculty members from a diversity of disciplines. It reviews most if not all courses offered on the campus and decides whether the courses meet often enough ("contact hours") and involve sufficient evaluation of students' performance and thus measure up to campus standards. The evident aim of such a committee is to safeguard academic quality.

- Ad hoc personnel committees, composed of members with a mix of disciplinary skills and experience, review and pass judgment on colleagues and recommend promotion, advancement, or some negative action to a dean or a provost. The objectives are to promote the quality of the faculty and to avoid arbitrariness and injustice in personnel matters.

- Sometimes an administrator will place "troubled" departments —usually the trouble is declining quality, internal conflict, or both—into receivership and appoint a special internal or external committee or commission to give advice on ways and means to improve the situation in the short and long run. I served as chair of such a committee on Harvard's sociology department for several years in the 1980s, offering periodic advice to the dean of the college and the president of the university. We focused above all on rebuilding the quality of the department.

- Many colleges and universities have a *committee on committees.* Such a committee is sometimes the butt of unkind jokes, representing, it is supposed, evidence of the absurdity of the principle of committee proliferation. Its main function, however— staffing all other committees with the most appropriate and best personnel—is consistent with the goals of enhancing the rationality and quality of an academic organization.

One must add immediately that these are intended functions; in practice any committee can perform well or badly in carrying them out. But as intended functions, they reveal what most academic committees are about.

The Committee as Umpire

All organizations, including academic ones, are riddled with internal conflicts. Academic backbiting and struggles over intellectual turf seem as incurable as they are notorious. This has led to the observation that there are no organizations in the world, except perhaps for monasteries and convents, that experience more political bickering than do colleges and universities. This seems odd, because so little power resides in academic organizations, and the political stakes of conflict in them are almost always low. Be that as it may, it is true that conflict is omnipresent in the academy. Another widely appreciated feature of organizations is that they tend to develop mazes of bureaucratic rules, regulations, and the accompanying red tape. We commonly attribute this to the sheer increase in size and functioning of an organization or to some sort of organizational pathology. An example of the latter is the famous "Parkinson's Law," which proclaims the universal tendency for organizations to develop into barnacled bureaucracies even when—or perhaps because—there is no additional work to be done.

What is less well understood, however, is the *connection* between organizational conflict and the growth of bureaucratic rules and regulations, as well as the central place that committees have in this connection. Here are two examples of the link:

- In the spring of 1992, when I was chair of the sociology department at Berkeley, my colleagues voted without opposition to appoint a candidate whom we regarded as the very best of 90 applicants for a junior faculty position in the area of race and ethnic relations. Immediately thereafter a group of graduate students raised a hot protest and called a one-week boycott of classes, because, among other reasons, that candidate was not a member of a minority group. The case was complicated by the fact that the successful candidate had applied well after the advertised deadline for applications. The campus administration voided the department's recommendation—even though we had given consideration to all late candidates—on grounds that we conceivably might have given the candidate an unequal advantage over others who might have applied late if they had known that they could have done so. But in the context of this complex conflict the administration discovered that it possessed no written rules regarding lateness of applications and no systematic way of discerning whether those candidates recommended by departments for appointment had applied on time or late. Thus was uncovered an embarrassing organizational ambiguity. In the aftermath the administration formed an informal committee, which ultimately came up with a definite rule that applications received after the advertised deadline would not be considered. Thus was born a new piece of organizational machinery designed to reduce ambiguity and the probability of future conflicts.

- Back in 1970, when the United States launched a military incursion into Cambodia, a national protest movement developed. The killings of students at Kent State University in Ohio and Jackson State University in Mississippi were dramatic and tragic moments in that protest. On the Berkeley campus the protest mainly took the form of a *reconstitution movement*—that is, to reconstitute classrooms and classes into protest groups to go out and do political work in the community. The movement generated great outrage among some parents, legislators, and members of the board of regents; feelings were especially inflamed toward faculty members who cooperated in the reconstitution of their classes. The legislature subsequently killed a cost-of-living increase for faculty, and pressure to discipline the faculty or increase its workload, or both, began to build. The president of the university threatened to promulgate a faculty code of conduct, and, using this threat, persuaded the academic senate to develop such a code. The senate responded by mobilizing a major committee, which drafted a code of faculty conduct that specified rules about teaching and meeting classes, stipulated sanctions for violators, and built in machinery for appeals for those charged with violating the code. The code was ultimately adopted by the university. It was meant to make explicit the rules that had previously been only taken-for-granted understandings, to build machinery for dealing with breaking the new rules, and to avoid future misunderstandings and conflicts. In this way the university built up its organizational complexity, and made use of the mechanism of the committee in doing so.

I daresay that if we examined the histories of all our institutions we would find the cycle of ambiguity, incident, conflict, committee activation, and new rules and regulations to be very pervasive.

The Committee as Unifier

Committees not only are nurtured by political conflict within organizations, but also serve to build consensus and incorporate opposition. Two examples demonstrate this.

* When I was on the Committee on Committees of the academic senate on the Berkeley campus in 1988-1989, we dealt almost exclusively with replacing academic senate committee members who had resigned or whose terms had expired, forming new committees, and providing slates of faculty members to administrators who wanted to staff committees. In all these matters we were forever preoccupied with the issue of "representativeness"—that is, securing representation from an array of academic disciplines: from professional schools as well as departments in the letters and sciences, from younger as well as older faculty, from minority as well as nonminority faculty members, and so on. Sometimes it seemed as though we had more categories to represent than we had members to appoint. In any event, while we were not always explicit on the matter, this concern with representativeness was a concern with more than tapping the best range of academic talent. It was a political concern: a concern simultaneously to incorporate actual and imagined constituencies into the action, to give them a modicum of power through representation, to make them part of the team, to make them responsible for the team's collective product, and to blunt potential criticisms from constituencies to the effect that they "had not been consulted."
* In the spring of 1991 I was asked by the chancellor to chair a blue-ribbon committee on intercollegiate athletics on the Berkeley campus, an arena fraught with a history of competition (among the empires of men's athletics, women's athletics, and recreational sports), long-standing alumni dissatisfaction with non-winning teams, and budgetary woes. The composition of the

committee was an ingenious political mix of old alumni blues of different stripes, faculty members, administrators and students, men and women, and seasoned and unseasoned people. We were also asked—if we did not know already—to consult with every known and imagined constituency interested in intercollegiate athletics. An evident but not always spoken function of the committee was to get as many constituencies as possible "on board" and thereby effect concerted action without undue opposition.

An interesting twist on the issue of political unity and loyalty is the well-known practice of *co-optation*. Put simply, co-optation means to invite known oppositionists into the camp by appointing them to a committee and thus making them, temporarily at least, a real or nominal part of the establishment. If successful, co-optation tames and civilizes the oppositions, brings them closer to an emerging consensus, and makes them responsible for that consensus. The practices of co-optation and assimilation are familiar mechanisms in American society, so much so that our society has been described as a "marshmallow cage" by critics. In any event, these practices are widespread as mechanisms in the committee life of academic institutions and must be understood as part and parcel of leaders' interest in consensus building and conflict management. Oppositions recognize this, of course, and are forever suspicious of co-optation. Moreover, the effort to co-opt can misfire, in ways that I will mention later.

The Committee as Rubber Stamp

One source of cynicism about the committee is that it is often regarded as a kind of pale substitute for decisive action, or, even more, a kind of inaction. The accusation is partly true, partly untrue. It is often true that an administrator stalls for time in a hot or troubled situation by appointing a committee to review the situation. It is also true that administrators may harbor the hope that, by burial in a committee, an issue may die of strangulation or fatigue. At the same time, to form a committee constitutes a kind of risk for the administrator. Charge it as specifically as he or she may, the act of appointing a committee endows that group with a certain independence, a certain unpredictability of outcome, a certain danger that it will uncover even deeper and more disturbing issues. The committee also sometimes serves to confirm and legitimize decisions already made. This is another common source of cynicism. Again there is both truth and untruth in the allegation. All of us on the blue-ribbon committee on intercollegiate athletics knew that the chancellor wanted to upgrade intercollegiate athletics on the Berkeley campus, and there was tacit agreement that we would operate under that constraint. We also knew that the chancellor was in all likelihood dissatisfied with the administrative separation of men's and women's athletics and wanted us to recommend their merger.

At the same time there are constraints on the use of the committee simply as an endorser of decisions already made. For one thing, the administrator faces limits on the degree to which he or she may dictate to committees. Detailed monitoring may generate feelings on the part of committee members that they are being used, and they may make these feelings public. In addition, an administrator is always vulnerable to the charge of "committee stacking," a charge that, if it sticks, can cost the administrator credibility and legitimacy.

The Committee as Competitor in the Power Game

The relations between committee activity and the process of decision making go beyond the possibilities of avoiding decisions and rubber-stamping. By forming a committee, an administrator sheds a measure of his or her authority by seeking advice. To form a committee is thus in one sense to diffuse power. At the same time, a committee typically does not make final decisions, only advises on them; the administrator retains final authority. This means that a committee, freed from final responsibility, can itself be freer in its deliberations and recommendations, because it is less directly involved with the constituencies whom its actions will affect than is the administrator, who is responsible for a final decision. Furthermore, when an administrative decision is finally made, it is possible for an administrator to avoid responsibility for the decision by claiming that he or she is following the advice of the committee and thus presumably representing the consensus it has reached. For its part, the committee can also avoid responsibility by claiming that, once its work is done, it is "discharged" and the responsibility for decisions lies with the administrator. The existence of a committee thus seems to permit disclaimers all around.

There are other possibilities as well. An administrator may make a decision other than that recommended by the committee, but claim that he or she is following its dictates. This possibility becomes all the more available when the committee's recommendations are vague, which they well may be if the committee is internally divided or produces a compromised "camel" in its report. Or, if the administrator finds the committee's work unacceptable, he or she may declare it so or call for more study and appoint another committee. All these possibilities—and probably more—are no doubt among the reasons why the committee is such a marvelous thing. It can be given an apparently critical role in the process of decision making while remaining in actuality a very ambiguous element in that process. In these ways it can help provide organizational leaders with the three things they value most: legitimacy, credibility, and flexibility.

Box 1.1 gives a shorthand summary of the main functions of committees. Needless to say, any given committee can perform many of them at the same time, and there is no contradiction involved in saying, for example, that a committee is simultaneously part of the conflict process and a political unifier. Furthermore, before deciding whether to serve on or chair a committee, you should try to find out what that committee is expected to do. For example, if you can determine that a committee is being formed simply to postpone decisive action or to rubber-stamp a fait accompli, you will likely not want to serve on it unless you agree with those particular administrative strategies. In practice, however, to find out what a projected committee is all about is easier said than done. Administrators are seldom fully forthcoming about the purposes of committees. They typically insist that the committee they want should be a collective thinker or an umpire, but they will seldom reveal any other political purposes out of a fear of making these purposes public and out of fear of demeaning the committee's independence and importance. As a result, finding out what an administrator expects of a committee often requires a lot of detective work.

A Jumble of Committee Types

The many functions of a committee differ in salience, depending on the type of committee. In the rest of the chapter I indicate the dimensions along which committees vary and say a few words about the kind of experience you may expect on the various types of committees. Needless to say, the typology is not entirely neat, because the dimensions overlap with one another.

Standing Versus One-Time Committees

Most faculty committees of academic senates are standing —that is, they enjoy an indefinite existence: for example, a Committee on Committees, Committee on Educational Policy, Committee on Academic Personnel, Committee on Academic Freedom, and Committee on Privilege and Tenure. So do many administrative committees such as a Committee on Buildings and Grounds and advisory committees in various policy areas. Standing committees are also found on boards of trustees: for example, an Audit Committee, a Nominations Committee, and a Finance Committee.

One-time committees are those that arise from the perception of a an organizational problem, conflict, or crisis. My service on a commission to review Berkeley's School of Education in the early 1980s arose from such a situation. The school had led a troubled existence for years, and the campus administration was at sea with respect to how to reform it. So was my service on the external advisory committee on the Department of Sociology at Harvard, which was having difficulty recruiting and retaining faculty and was fraught with internal conflicts. The original reason for the formation of the Committee on Basic Research in the Behavioral and Social Sciences (National Research Council and National Academy of Sciences) in 1979 was to develop a reasoned response to congressional and other criticisms that basic research in the social sciences was insignificant, useless, or dangerous ideologically. (That committee lasted 8 years, however, and almost became a standing committee.) Other committees are partly standing and partly one-time, as, for example, are the committees that review academic departments in universities every 5 years or so.

As a general rule, you will find work on standing committees more predictable than on one-time or periodic committees. After all, their "standingness" derives from the fact that they are meant to handle recurring, even routine matters or issues. A committee on committees, for example, does almost nothing but staff or give recommendations for staffing other committees. A committee on educational policy mainly "reviews reviews"—that is, it receives and evaluates the reports of other committees that have evaluated academic units. By the same token, the work of standing committees is also the most boring of all committee work, simply because it is routine. My production of doodled-on Styrofoam cups has always been very high on standing committees. There are a few exceptions to this general rule, however. For years the Berkeley academic senate had a standing policy committee, a body that emerged out of the turbulent years of the 1960s. It was a committee explicitly designed to deal with breaking or looming issues and crises on the campus. Because that group did important work on important matters, it enjoyed high prestige, and being on it was usually challenging and enjoyable.

Committees on Policies Versus Committees on People and Their Work

The senate policy committee dealt with policies; so did the committee on intercollegiate athletics; so did the commission to evaluate the School of Education on the Berkeley campus. By contrast, ad hoc personnel committees are typically three- or five-person groups appointed to evaluate and make recommendations about a faculty member who is up for appointment or promotion; search committees also evaluate the careers and promise of applicants for faculty positions, deanships, presidencies, or directors of research units.

There are also standing committees that focus on people and their work. Every campus of the University of California has a committee on academic personnel (CAP) that reviews all important—and sometimes *all*—recommendations for new faculty appointments, merit increases, and promotions. Another example is the editorial board of the University of California Press, which reviews all manuscripts recommended to it by the editors of the press. The recommendations of the CAPs are advisory to the administration but are almost always followed by it. The recommendations of the editorial committee of the University of California Press are final.

Policy- and people-evaluating committees differ greatly from one another. Committees charged to deal with policies are usually not secretive, and, by virtue of their charge, are focused and instrumental in their work and culture. The standing committee that evaluates people and their work is usually more fascinating. Most of its work is secret, dealing as it does with confidential letters of recommendations, reports, and reviews of manuscripts. Its work, moreover, clearly affects the fortunes and careers of the people evaluated. Members of such a standing committee usually find their work important and like it. They have high morale. They develop strong, respectful, sometimes tribal feelings toward one another; as we say nowadays, they "bond together." They often maintain friendships with one another long after their terms of service have ended. And, as often as not, they develop a curiously arrogant culture, believing steadfastly that they do not make mistakes in judgment. We do not understand much about why these features develop, but they seem to be regular features of standing committees that assess colleagues and their work.

Goal-Specific Versus Advisory Committees

This is really a continuum rather than a dichotomy. A search committee for a dean has a single and definite charge—to find the best person—and, unless it is instructed to do otherwise, carries out nothing but this task. Another highly specific committee I once served on was one of the most unusual in my experience. It was called the Committee on Pieces of Paper. It was appointed back in the 1960s by a new Berkeley chancellor who wanted to know what kind of written messages students and faculty receive during the course of the academic year from the registrar's office, libraries, and the College of Letters and Science, to say nothing of the chancellor's office itself. We were asked to read all these pieces of paper—these official communications—from the standpoint of their informativeness, their level of interest, their friendliness or abusiveness, and their literary style. We found out how tedious and punitive most official campus communications actually are—for example, warning students in strident language that if they do not pay every nickel of their library fines they will never graduate. After we finished our survey we made several forceful recommendations for improvement. As far as I could determine, the committee's work had no impact whatsoever on any paper-producing agency on the campus, despite the ingeniousness of the idea.

Moving along the continuum, we find examples of committees with extremely broad charges. The Task Force on Lower

Division Education in the University of California, which carried out its work in 1985-1986, was given several specific questions to deal with, such as the ease or difficulty of transferring into the university from a community college and the role of teaching assistants, but most of the questions asked in the charge were very general; in the end it became apparent that the task force could have addressed almost any issue it chose. The Committee on Basic Research in the Behavioral and Social Sciences, in its 1980-1982 incarnation, was asked to write on the value, utility, and significance of the vast range of academics that fall under the range of "behavioral and social sciences," a seemingly inexhaustible charge. The most general-purpose of all committees are those chosen as informal advisory "kitchen cabinets" of powerful political and administrative leaders, groups that are called upon as sounding boards for any issues the leaders might have at hand. Such committees are usually very engaging because of their closeness to the seats of power, the diversity of their work, and the help and protection they afford leaders.

One could go on spinning out different kinds of committees—formal versus informal, advisory versus final decision making, and so on—but enough has been said to indicate their diversity, their relative importance, the different demands they place on their members, the types of participation required, and the kinds of commitment and morale they engender.

If you are a young faculty member, you should expect to be asked initially to serve on the least rewarding kinds of committees: standing committees that deal with routine and not very important matters. The underlying logic for this is found in the often implicit assumption that people early in their careers need "seasoning" in lesser committee work before taking on major assignments. (Some universities also operate on the assumption that young faculty members should be "protected" from demanding—and usually interesting— committee service so they can develop their scholarly careers at the pretenure stage.) This practice is unfortunate in a way, because minor, processing committees are the most boring and are likely to create a permanent distaste for committee work. The only cheerful counsel to be given to the young in this regard is to be patient, because if you perform effectively and responsibly at this level, more interesting assignments may lie ahead.

The most powerful and personally rewarding kinds of committees—people-evaluating committees and important policy committees and blue-ribbon commissions—are mainly populated with more senior faculty. With respect to people-evaluating committees, most colleges and universities work on the assumption that people of lower rank should be evaluated by people of higher rank and that such evaluation requires experience and discretion. Seasoned people are also found in greater numbers on major, one-time policy committees and commissions that focus on big problems or crises. The logic behind this is that the administrators who create such committees usually want them led by experienced, prestigious, and trusted members—people who will give greater legitimacy to the decisions that the administrators ultimately make in connection with the committee recommendations. One may challenge the validity of the assumptions that produce such a high correlation between seniority and gratifying committee assignments, but those assumptions seem to possess a certain sacredness and intractability in the academic world.

2 | Giving Birth to Committees

Before you agree to serve on a committee, you should reflect on two matters: (a) how and why the committee came into existence, and (b) why you might or might not want to serve on it. Those two matters are closely connected, and they are the subject of this chapter. I consider first the reasons for forming committees; second, the "charge," or the motive imparted to a committee; third, the selection of members for a committee; and finally, the motives you might have for joining a committee.

Forming a Committee

Permanent Committees

Most American colleges and universities have a roster of committees that are much the same as those in all other such institutions. There are administrative committees that deal with such issues as student conduct and misconduct, buildings and grounds, intercollegiate athletics, affirmative action, and sexual harassment. Faculty committees deal with academic personnel, academic planning, academic freedom, admissions, courses, prizes and fellowships, educational policy, faculty welfare, and privilege and tenure. Departments and schools

Box 2.1

Campus Needs and Committees to Meet Them

Maintaining academic quality
Examples: Personnel committees, committees on courses

Maintaining orderly bureaucratic functioning
Examples: Buildings and grounds committees, committees on academic planning

Adding or replacing personnel
Examples: Admissions committees, search committees

Setting and maintaining standards of conduct
Examples: Student conduct committees, committees on sexual harassment

Attending to issues of equity and justice
Examples: Committees on faculty welfare, committees on academic freedom

have undergraduate curriculum, graduate curriculum, graduate admissions, graduate evaluation, and personnel committees, and perhaps small committees on computing and on lectures and colloquia. Most campuses also make use of ad hoc personnel and search committees.

The reason for the similarities lies in the fact that these committees are lodged in a definite type of organizations: academic colleges and universities. These organizations have either continuing or recurring needs to attend to the same kinds of functions or problems. These needs, with appropriate committee illustrations, are shown in Box 2.1.

The circumstances of birth and renewal of this great array of committees are routine and largely uninteresting. (Staffing them is interesting, and I will speak of that momentarily.)

They are appointed by the administration, the academic senate committee on committees, or the departmental chair on a recurrent, usually annual, basis or when a vacancy for an administrative or faculty position occurs.

Special Committees

More interesting stories develop when we turn to committees that are formed to deal with problems or crises. Such committees often have special names to designate their special importance. They are called *task forces* ("task farces" by cynics), special advisory committees, blue-ribbon committees, or commissions—all signifying that they are more important than run-of-the-mill committees. These kinds of special committees have become a more important feature of college and university life than they once were, largely because those institutions have changed their character.

In the past several decades college and university life has become more of a public fishbowl; as such, it is now more likely to be involved in controversy and conflict. In that earlier time campuses enjoyed a great degree of privacy, isolation, and uncritical public support or at least tolerance; as a consequence, campuses enjoyed control over their own affairs. This partly imagined past was also an era of faculty control over one another through the mechanism of informal collegiality, as well as administrative and faculty control over students through the mechanism of diffuse authority known as *in loco parentis*. The main "incidents" in this era were breaches of the academic freedom of faculty members, moral scandals such as spouse stealing on the part of administrators and faculty, and infractions relating to "beer, cheating, and sex" for students.

All that has changed. The college and university—especially the major research university—has become larger, more complex, and, above all, more subject to public scrutiny under new standards of accountability. What might have passed unnoticed in the era of public ignorance is now noticed and aired by whole armies of new groups with new expectations and interests: government funding agencies; groups with environmental, health, and safety concerns; animal rights groups; parents who pay higher fees; racial and ethnic groups who wish to gain or have gained access; employee (including faculty) unions and associations; community leaders and interest groups; and, above all, the mass media.

With so many eyes on colleges and universities, and so many different expectations and demands brought to bear on them, they have become more visible and vulnerable. The number and kinds of potential "incidents," problems, and crises have multiplied, and the level of discomfort and mayhem in the lives of college and university officials has risen accordingly. Conflict and litigiousness appear to be the business of the day. College and university officials dread the constant threat of adverse publicity and do all they can to avoid it. I have often teased the public information officers of the Berkeley campus by telling them that their main function is to keep the university out of the news.

Regarding colleges and universities historically, we may note further that they have been well equipped to process individuals and individual behavior but ill equipped to handle groups and group conflicts. They admit individual students, test and grade them as individuals, discipline them as individuals, and graduate them as individuals. They know and are comfortable with individual academic competition as a way of life. They are not so comfortable with groups. One of the most unsettling features of the campus turmoil of the 1960s—the rallies, demonstrations, sit-ins, marches, and civil disobedience—was that it was *collective* in nature, and campus officials neither knew how nor had the machinery to deal with this collective dimension.

Since that time there has been a great deal of organizational learning on the part of officials and an improvement in their ability to handle group conflict. On the Berkeley campus, for example, there is a little-publicized group called, informally and simply, "The Committee." It is headed by an assistant to the chancellor and has student affairs personnel, deans of student conduct, campus police officials, and public information officers as members. The committee is a kind of permanently established firehouse brigade with a mission to anticipate and track potential political conflict situations and to deal with them effectively when they arise. Despite this kind of learning and invention, colleges and universities typically lag behind on this score and are thus vulnerable to surprises. Correspondingly, they frequently respond to surprises in ad hoc ways by forming committees to deal with problems. Such are some of the dynamics that have led to the honeycombing of academic life with ever-increasing numbers and types of special committees.

Special committees often develop as a result of some dramatic incident: a football scandal, a rash of rapes on campus, a dramatic drinking or drug incident that results in a death, a racial clash, an unanticipated student protest, the exposure of some university practice in its laboratory research on animals. Such incidents typically create an outcry in some quarter, and a frequent reaction on the part of college and university officials is to activate an existing committee or form a new one to investigate, review, and make recommendations. On other occasions special committees are formed in response to persistent criticism or recognition of a growing problem or crisis.

Let me illustrate this process by turning to the Task Force on Lower-Division Education in the University of California, which I chaired and which did its work during the 1985-86 academic year. The early 1980s witnessed one of those periodic episodes of external criticism and internal soul-searching about the value and effectiveness of the American system of collegiate education. Three prestigious national organizations —the National Endowment of the Humanities, the National Institute of Education, and the Association of American

Colleges—launched separate commissions and issued major reports within a year of one another. The tone of the reports was uniformly dire, and menacing phrases occurred regularly: "chronic paralysis," "unhappy disarray," "loss of integrity," "vacuum of educational leadership," and "failure of nerve." The reports attracted a great deal of attention in the national press, and many citizens assumed that a genuine crisis in undergraduate education was at hand.

This aura of crisis seeped into California political and educational circles as well, feeding into long-standing concerns about the mission and performance of the University of California in the area of undergraduate education. The university, being financially supported by the state, has always been supposed to provide high-quality undergraduate education for a sizeable talented elite of California's young people. However, a kind of chronic nervousness about the university's performance as an undergraduate institution had developed over the years. This nervousness can be traced mainly to the facts that the system had become huge and that it had diverted its energies to becoming one of the leading research and graduate-training institutions in the world. While very proud of the record on the latter front, groups of California politicians and citizens have given more or less continuous expression to dozens of misgivings: too much emphasis on research, too little on teaching; large, poorly scheduled, and inaccessible classes; too much use of temporary faculty; too much use of graduate-student teaching assistants, many of whom are foreign and cannot teach in English; low quality of instruction and advising; too much bureaucracy; too much waiting in lines; impersonality; alienation; and on and on.

Within California higher education itself, representatives from the other educational segments—the California State University system and the community college system—were ready enough to join the chorus of critical voices, claiming implicitly that they, not the University of California, were the state's premier undergraduate educational institutions. The evident continuing popularity of the university, expressed in enormous numbers of applications to enroll and very high levels of student satisfaction, did not seem to cool the fire of criticism, which was further fueled by the national concern with undergraduate education in the early 1980s.

The president of the university, David Gardner, an inventive leader, decided to take the initiative in the area of undergraduate education, about which the university's posture had traditionally been of a defensive quality. His strategy was to form a special type of committee. It was to be called a task force, thus giving it an edge of special meaning. It was to limit itself to the lower division—the freshman and sophomore—years that were widely regarded as fraught with the educational woes of massiveness, impersonality, and faculty neglect. The task force was to address all the major points of criticism head on. It was to be chaired by a faculty member and populated mainly with faculty members, thus symbolizing the commitment of those in the university who were most responsible for students' education. And above all, the task force was to demonstrate that the university itself was taking the lead in this troublesome arena, with the not-so-implicit footnote that, because it was doing so, the state legislature and other interested parties would have no legitimate basis for intervening.

Such were the political circumstances of the birth of the Task Force on Lower-Division Education in the University of California. These circumstances were, of course, not the only context in which that awkwardly named committee was significant; it makes sense for an organization to assess its missions from time to time, especially in periods of change. But the formation of the committee—as well as its charge, its work, and its products—cannot be fathomed or appreciated without a knowledge of the surrounding political circumstances. The committee's members, above all others, had to understand these circumstances in order to know what they were about and to fashion their work accordingly.

Charging the Committee

The *charge*—which gives a committee its official direction —is a standard feature of all committees. The charge is implicit for some committees and explicit for others. In almost all cases, however, a charge reveals several agendas, some of which are latent. Both the writing and reading of charges are thus special art forms and must be appreciated by those who serve on committees.

Standard Charges

Most routine committees in colleges and universities need no charge, even though such a charge may be written down somewhere and made available to new members on a periodic basis. The reason for this is that the charge is self-evident through familiarity and common knowledge. If you are appointed to the Committee on Public Ceremonies, for example, it does not take much imagination to figure out that the duties are to advise the administration on participants, protocol, and procedures for largely traditional and fixed rituals. Similarly, a member of the Committee on Faculty Welfare knows, without being specially instructed, that it deals with issues having to do with medical and insurance plans, retirement benefits, and general levels of remuneration. The main reason for having the seldom-read charges in existence is to provide some kind of constitutional reference point to be consulted when ambiguities about the committee's jurisdiction over a given situation or issue arise.

Personnel search committees can also usually operate without a specific written charge. They are supposed to search for the best individual for a designated job, and they do not need to be told this. (Most of the instructions to search committees now concern the issue of how to search—that is, what kind of advertising, evaluation, and interviewing procedures should be followed to make the search fair and in keeping with affirmative action guidelines.) When charges for search committees are written down, moreover, they often drift toward meaninglessness, because they all turn out to be much the same and equally impossible to realize. Practically every search for a university chancellor or president, for example, stipulates that the successful candidate have an outstanding academic background, possess administrative and other organizational experience, have diplomatic skills, be flexible but decisive, be able to show sympathy and listen but also be independent, and all the rest. Inevitably such lists of criteria call forth cynical comments about "superperson" or "walk on water" from members. Moreover, the criteria listed often lose force and devolve into a general checklist at best when the committee actually gets down to the work of evaluating candidates.

Special Committees

The most interesting charges are those given to committees formed to deal with problems arising from organizational ambiguity, controversy, or conflict. The main reason for the necessity of a charge in these instances, of course, is that the committee is being formed anew, and must be told what is expected of it in a nonroutine situation. It needs marching orders. Such an observation, however, constitutes only the tip of the iceberg. There are other dimensions to the charge, and its tacit, unwritten ingredients are often more important than that which is written down literally. To illustrate its subtleties, I will first identify a few general rules of thumb about the charge, with examples, and then examine in more detail the charge to the Task Force on Lower-Division Education.

If you are asked to serve on a special committee, there are several principles to keep in mind in interpreting its charge:

- Be certain to identify the manifest areas of central concern to the committee. This is perhaps too obvious to mention, and it is included only for the sake of completeness. When the chancellor of the Berkeley campus charged his blue-ribbon committee on intercollegiate athletics in 1991, he asked us to report on the institutional mission of intercollegiate athletics, to address the question of to whom should coaches and athletic directors report administratively, and to pay special attention to budgetary constraints. Then he mentioned, somewhat casually, several areas that were "bound to be of interest to the committee," including the relations between men's and women's athletics and the problem of athletic facilities and their maintenance.

* Recognize that there are open-ended opportunities in the charge. Intelligent administrators appreciate that a committee has a mind of its own—or is sure to develop one if it is told not to—and cannot be forced to regard the charge as exhaustive. In charging the athletics committee, the chancellor did not specify the problems relating to the student athlete or to faculty involvement in intercollegiate athletics. It was tacitly understood, however, that the committee, almost half of whose members were faculty members, might (and did ultimately) address these two issues in its report.

* Recognize that a charge is almost always framed in general terms, so that the committee may begin at square one. The chancellor did that in his charge to the athletics committee when he asked for a statement of general mission for intercollegiate athletics. Two reasons lie behind this feature of the committee charge. First, administrators prefer to define concrete, immediate problems in generic, broad, and timeless terms, in part because they do not feel comfortable in acknowledging that a troublesome situation constitutes a crisis. To do so is to admit organizational failure, and organizational failure signals administrative failure, which in turn suggests personal failure. Second, faculty members on committees will go to square one in their discussions anyway, no matter what they have been asked to do. I have served on curriculum committees that have considered matters so minute as changing a word or two in the title of a required course, and I have invariably witnessed nothing less than a full-scale philosophical debate on the fundamentals of education before the wording issue is resolved. This seems to constitute a central character trait (or flaw) of faculty members, and it brings to mind the observation that if academics are ever to die from anything, it will be from too much talking.

- Look for unrevealed political agendas in the charge. When the officials of the National Academy of Sciences and the National Research Council wrote the charge to its Committee on Basic Research in the Behavioral and Social Sciences in 1989, they explained that they were asking the committee, "at the request of the National Science Foundation," to assess the value, significance, and social utility of basic research. Behind this benign request lay a history of attacks on social science research by Senator William Proxmire (D.-Wisconsin) and others in the U.S. Congress and the looming menace to social-science research found in the rhetoric of President Ronald Reagan and David Stockman, his budget director. The import of these attacks was that basic research in the social sciences is without value, insignificant if not trivial, and socially useless if not ideologically threatening. But the committee charge and the committee report took the high road, and the partisan struggle underlying the committee's work was thus obscured. Also, when the Berkeley chancellor asked us to consider the relations between men's and women's athletics and the administrative reporting relationships of athletic directors and coaches, this language concealed a long history of competition and infighting between men's and women's athletics, and a chaotic history of athletic directors and coaches "jumping" the administrative line in an effort to gain the chancellor's ear.

These rules of thumb reveal that special committees created to meet problems or crises operate on at least two levels and that—in a kind of unconscious conspiracy with their administrative creators—respect the line between those levels. The real "problems" that constitute the true basis for the committee's charge are to be found in the organizational trenches, with all their complexities, strains, and political struggles. The explicit charge to a committee, however, elevates these concrete situations and struggles to a more general and benign level, at which the committee proceeds. Furthermore, the committee in its turn supplies the administrator with general language and options that may be used—as a kind of resource given legitimacy by committee endorsement—to return to the organizational trenches and to try to restore order through negotiation and decision making.

Such a conspiracy is useful because it simultaneously permits the administrator to "rise above" the conflict and provides him or her with both language and legitimacy to deal with the conflict. It might even be said that successful committee work depends on a tacit agreement between both committee and administration to proceed according to the terms of this conspiracy. The successful organizational committee, moreover, is one that understands both the manifest (general) agenda given in its charge and the latent (political) charge implied by it. If that conspiracy backfires in any way—for example, if the committee becomes completely partisan— then a new range of political problems appears for the administrator.

To close out this line of thinking, Box 2.2 shows the charge given to the Task Force on Lower-Division Education in 1985 as the university faced the practical and political situation outlined in the last section.

That charge presented the task force with one immediate problem: It was impossibly long and cluttered. In some cases the questions were so general and required so much empirical information as to demand half a book to answer them— for example, the question relating to the appropriate level of resources for lower-division education. To have dealt with all of the issues would have yielded too many words and too many recommendations, each of which constitutes a kind of kiss of death for committee reports (more on this in Chapter 6). The task force ultimately solved this problem by ignoring nearly half the questions in the charge.

The charge also illustrates all the rules of thumb I have enunciated about reading charges. The entire statement was developed in the form of questions—not statements—which is a way of pinpointing general issues but not suggesting specific solutions. Moreover, the questions were phrased in soft if not bland language. Virtually all the topics and questions—

Box 2.2

Charge to the Task Force on
Lower-Division Education

The task force is to address the following issues:
1. The nature of the University's mission in lower-division education.
   _____ What is the importance of lower-division education to the University's teaching mission?
   _____ Are the resources devoted to lower-division education appropriate?
2. The nature and quality of the lower-division curriculum.
   _____ Are the campus's current general education requirements adequate? Should there be a common lower-division curriculum for the University as a whole? For each campus?
   _____ What should be the balance between courses taken to fulfill general education requirements and those taken as prerequisites to the major?
   _____ Are current procedures for periodic review of the curriculum adequate?
3. The quality of teaching and learning.
   _____ Are courses needed for general education requirements and prerequisites for the major available to all freshman and sophomore students in the proper sequence? How do campuses respond to changes in student demand?

particularly those under the first heading—invited the task force to begin at the square one of educational philosophy and principles. The whole charge has an air of academic neutrality about it, and reading it on its face (both then and now)

_____ What is the optimum balance among types of courses —i.e., seminars, lectures—for the student's first two years in the University? Is an appropriate balance of courses available to all students?

_____ Who teaches lower-division courses? What is the appropriate balance between full-time/part-time, tenure track/nontenure track?

_____ What is the appropriate role for teaching assistants? Are TAs adequately trained and supervised?

_____ Should lower-division students have greater opportunities to work with senior faculty? If so, how might this be accomplished?

_____ How should learning be assessed?

_____ How can high-quality teaching be recognized and rewarded? Are current practices sufficient?

4. Academic support services (academic advising and learning skills programs).

_____ Should there be University-wide objectives for advising lower-division students?

_____ How is academic advising handled on the campuses? What is the faculty's role? Is the advising system effective?

_____ What is the role of learning skills programs, such as tutoring, in educating lower-division students? Are these programs effective?

one would scarcely guess that the charge reflected a range of political issues ranging from lukewarm to hot.

If one is aware of the context and reads between the lines, however, it is possible to discern the unspoken political agenda. The first item under the third heading, for example, uses the word *available* with respect to freshman and sophomore courses; this is a kind of code word for the major complaint among freshmen and sophomores—and their parents—that large introductory courses were hopelessly overcrowded in many instances, and that throngs of students could not take the courses they wanted when they wanted them. The second item under the third heading raised the thorny issue of class size and impersonality. The third and fourth items reflected the accusations of faculty irresponsibility—that is, do they turn over lower division teaching to temporarily appointed lecturers and teaching assistants? But, as indicated, a naive reading of the questions would regard them as queries relating to educational and pedagogical principles and practice.

Other political sore spots were addressed even more obliquely. The naive reader will note that the issue of racial and ethnic access to the university does not appear in the charge, even though that issue was alive in 1985 and both access and diversity evidently affect undergraduate education. (Actually, the task force did recommend further diversification and internationalization of the undergraduate curriculum in its final report, even though it was not asked to address the matter in the charge.) The last item in the charge, which refers to "learning skills programs," is largely an issue touching on remedial work for minority students with disadvantaged educational backgrounds. The question of the resources dedicated to such programs was an issue in which minorities have a direct interest.

The issue of minority access also lurked—though even further in the background—behind the first item under the second heading, which asked whether there should be a common general education curriculum for all campuses. The connection was this: In 1985 the numbers of students transferring to the University of California from community colleges had been shrinking for more than a decade and had reached a figure of about 5,000 a year. This trend opened the issue of minority access, because such a high proportion of community college students is composed of minorities. A decline of transfer rates would appear to have an adverse effect on minority access to the university. Furthermore, some critics attributed the falling rates to the university's labyrinthine system of course requirements in general education necessary for transfer students, which differed from campus to campus and seemed an obstacle to those wishing to transfer. Would not a common core curriculum for general education throughout the University of California ease the process and encourage more transfers?

On still other topics the charge was silent. The most notable of these was faculty research activity and its relation to lower-division teaching. The only hint appeared in the last item under the third heading, which refers to the recognition and reward of high-quality lower-division teaching. The questions could be taken to imply that lower-division teaching is undervalued. But that is the only hint. In a way the omission is curious, because in the minds of many critics the great priority given by faculty to research was the chief cause of the suspected deterioration of undergraduate education. I never came to know the reasons for the omission, but I suspect that the issue of research versus teaching would have proven too divisive and opened too many unwelcome cans of worms both inside and outside the university.

To sum up, it can be argued that the charge to a one-time, problem-addressing or crisis-meeting committee is, ironically, both an important and an incomplete feature of committee work. It is important that such a committee have a charge. It is important that the charge be recognized as a kind of "high road" document that avoids direct recognition of organizational conflict or crisis or else approaches that aspect in an oblique, crablike fashion. Moreover, it is important for you, as a committee member, to know the political conditions surrounding the formation and existence of the committee. Finally, however, it is equally important to know that you do not learn everything about these political conditions by reading its charge.

Staffing the Committee:
The Art of the Possible

If you spend your life as an academic, you may not have too many opportunities to appoint committees. You will do so if you serve as chair of your academic department. Also, some of you will move into the part-time or full-time administration, and you will discover that a sizable part of the business of deans and provosts is to appoint committees. Even if you are only on the receiving end of committee appointments, however, it is helpful to know about some basic principles of staffing.

Having served as chair of the Department of Sociology at Berkeley on two occasions, I have staffed its committees several times. These committees, it will be remembered, are graduate admissions, personnel, graduate curriculum, and the like. Ideally, one approaches this task in a rational way, getting the best people to do the appropriate jobs. It does not work out that way, however, for two reasons:

❶ Some colleagues find committee work distasteful and do whatever they can to get out of it. Others are incompetent or nonresponsible. When these facts are added to the annual round of sabbatical and other leaves, a chair finds that the major problem is finding enough able and willing bodies to do the work. It is another back-against-the-wall situation for the chair, who often settles for less just to keep the work flowing. As a potential departmental committee member, you should realize this and know that the chair is often willing to negotiate with you over particular committee assignments because he or she is so hard-pressed to get all of them filled from a small reservoir of willing hands.

❷ Sometimes faculty members care about the kind of power that a committee exercises. This frequently happens in one type of committee: that responsible for evaluating colleagues for promotion or recruiting new ones. Department faculties are likely to have the strongest feelings and experience the deepest divisions in these personnel cases. In forming committees for these cases, an effect different from reluctance to serve sometimes arises. Some colleagues may want to serve on personnel committees or at least have their political allies serve on them. In such cases the chair is called upon to exercise political as well as administrative skills and attend to balancing political constituencies as well as knowledge of specialized areas of the discipline on personnel committees.

Speaking more generally, it is a kind of rule that when committee work is routine and noncontroversial, the main burden that falls on the one who appoints is to be able to round up the less-than-willing troops to do the chores. In my experience with the Committee on Committees of the Berkeley Academic Senate, the principal task in forming routine committees is to find a cadre of people who are (a) competent, (b) at least minimally experienced, (c) not on leave, (d) endowed with a civil or at least not disagreeable personal style, and (e) willing to serve. If all those criteria are applied, the pool sometimes becomes small.

Inevitably, however, political considerations enter in. As indicated, the Committee on Committees is forever preoccupied with balance. In fact, that committee might be regarded as one of the most politically sensitive committees of the entire campus, because it is responsible for staffing all the others. It is the only elected committee in the entire Academic Senate. One could argue that it is elected because there is no other way to appoint it as parent of all other committees. That argument is not sufficient, however, because other mechanisms, such as appointment by the chair of the entire senate, could be envisioned. My own belief is that it is elected by the voting faculty because it is political and needs an elected status to carry out its work freely and with legitimacy.

Achieving balance in the staffing of a committee is a delicate art. In selecting senate committees, the Committee on Committees keeps several categories implicitly and often explicitly in mind. Among these are the following:

age and experience versus "new blood"; assistant professors are generally excluded from committee work, consideration

---

Box 2.3

**Members of the Task Force
on Lower-Division Education**

The following members are categorized by their professional status, area of academic expertise, campus, and gender and ethnicity.

_____ University professor (that is, a professor of the entire University of California system), sociologist, Berkeley campus, white male, as chair

_____ Provost and professor of chemistry, San Diego campus, white male

_____ Professor of religious studies, Santa Barbara campus, white male

_____ Lecturer in English, Irvine campus, white female

_____ Provost and associate professor of mathematics, Santa Cruz campus, white male

_____ Professor and chair of history, Riverside campus, Hispanic male

_____ Visiting lecturer in French, Santa Cruz campus, white female

_____ Undergraduate student representative from student government, Los Angeles campus, Hispanic male

---

usually being given to the importance of research at this stage in their careers;

professional schools versus letters and science faculty membership;

gender;

minority status;

known positions or "stands" on important campus and political issues in the past;

_____ Staff member, president's office, white female

_____ Professor of engineering, Santa Barbara campus, Asian female

_____ Professor of political science and dean of undergraduate studies, Berkeley campus, white male

_____ Dean, College of Letters and Science, professor of sociology, Davis campus, white male

_____ Associate vice president of academic affairs, president's office, white male

_____ Professor of history, Los Angeles campus, white male

_____ Professor of biomathematics and director of the honors program, Los Angeles campus, white female

_____ Associate professor of religious studies, Riverside campus, white female

_____ Visiting lecturer in rhetoric, Davis campus, white female

_____ Associate professor of German and director of film studies, Irvine campus, white male

_____ Vice chancellor of undergraduate affairs and professor of chemistry, San Diego campus, black male

_____ Graduate student and teaching assistant in English, Berkeley campus, white female

reputation as a "committee member" in terms of attendance, responsibility, conscientiousness, and so on;

service in the recent past—the balance between relying on a tried and true committee member versus the norm against overworking and relying on a small cadre of "old senate hands."

The several criteria assume different salience with respect to different committees, but none is ever entirely absent.

The more important and potentially controversial a committee, the more important it is to ensure its legitimacy by achieving a balance of known or imagined constituencies. If the constituencies are many and salient, moreover, the task demands a certain amount of wizardry. The Task Force on Lower-Division Education again provides a ready example. Because of the special political significance of the task force with respect to external audiences, it was important *not* to select members of the task force who were themselves as critical as outsiders of the university's undergraduate programs. At the same time it was important to select members who would be sufficiently reflective so as to avoid producing either a defensive or a "whitewash" document. And those selected had to have a known reputation for being good undergraduate teachers, for administering programs in undergraduate education, for developing innovative programs or courses, or at the very least, for being sympathetic to and not arrogant about the education of freshmen and sophomores. Meeting these desiderata required a good deal of guesswork because the president's office, which appointed the task force, had limited information about the faculty and administrative staff of all its campuses. (It was a universitywide, eight-campus task force; the San Francisco campus was excluded on grounds that it has no undergraduate programs.) Also, the president's office had only limited time and capacity to consult about the optimum membership.

In addition to these general criteria, the president's office had to do the usual balancing with respect to constituencies *within* the university. Each campus had to be represented, and faculty (both regular and temporary), administrators, students, and staff were needed as well. By 1985, moreover, no responsible staffer of committees could be insensitive to the issues of gender, race, and ethnicity. The list of members of that task force, designated by relevant labels, is shown in Box 2.3. Inspection reveals the categories that were juggled to attain the politically appropriate kind of mix on the committee.

Meeting those needs of representativeness yielded a task force of 20 members, a number that pressed the limits of committee workability. Furthermore, it was now expected that this group of 20—highly diversified on many counts, mostly strangers to one another, working in the complex political environment described—would gather together periodically for six months or so and produce a coherent and effective statement on lower-division education in the University of California as a whole. Described as such, the job of the task force seems impossible. It was not, however, and that fact testifies to the strength of the common academic and committee cultures that virtually all the members brought to the task force.

The Chair

Two more items on staffing merit mentioning. The first is selecting a chair. This varies in importance, as do most other aspects of committee work. For routine committee work, a hard-working person who keeps the work flowing and committee members involved and working is sufficient. For the more complex committee that must swim in political waters, the selection of a chair can be the most important single act of the committee's history. The many reasons for this will become clear in the discussion of effective chairing in Chapter 5.

Co-optation

Earlier I mentioned co-optation, the second issue, as an aspect of the political significance of committees. The administrator who constitutes a committee must strive to attain a mix of members who can develop a common committee culture and cooperate to produce a consensual and reasonably acceptable report. If he or she follows only this dictate, however, the result is likely to be a committee that lacks legitimacy because it is too homogeneous, too friendly to the administrator, and not representative enough. At the very least the administrator must strive for diversity and the presence of most if not all interested constituencies.

If he or she wishes to push this principle further, the administrator can resort to co-optation, or the recruitment of representatives of known opposition groups, in the hope that they will be won over by responsible involvement in the committee work and by being drawn closer to the center of administrative power. Moreover, if representatives of the opposition can be persuaded to support a collective committee consensus, any criticism they might express of that consensus in the future will likely be tinged with a lack of credibility. The principle of co-optation is always filled with risk, however. When I was chair of the systemwide Academic Senate of the University of California in 1987, the chronic and intractable issue of the university's relationship to the Livermore and Los Alamos weapons laboratories came into high salience, as it does every five years when the university's board of regents renegotiates the laboratories' contracts between the U.S. Department of Defense, which owns and supports the laboratories, and the university, which oversees their scientific programs. Faculty feelings ran high this year, and opinions ranged from full support of the university's involvement as an aspect of public service all the way to moral indignation over the university's compliance with the defense establishment and the nuclear war machine.

In the course of debate and discussion, the academic council of the senate—which I chaired—was persuaded to form a committee that was to report 2½ years hence on the feasibility of continuing the university's relationship with the laboratories. I was assigned to appoint that committee. Relying in part on the advice of others, I appointed two known crusaders against the university's laboratory involvement to the committee in hopes that they would be co-opted into a reasonable, consensual, informed, not either-or statement after their years of work. My judgment proved wrong, and my hopes were ultimately dashed. A cooperative spirit never developed, the two continued to campaign within the committee, the committee polarized frequently, and in the end it produced a report that was acceptable to only part of the committee. In this case the strategy of co-optation misfired, and the committee operated mainly as a microcosm of the larger conflict within the faculty as a whole. Not everyone considered the committee's work a failure, however, and perhaps no committee could have written a report and made recommendations that would have gained consensus, so deep ran the divisions over the weapons laboratories. In any event, the episode illustrates how indistinct and difficult is the path between the involvement of diverse constituencies on one hand and unsuccessful co-optation on the other.

Staffing Committees: Why Do People (and Why Should You) Serve?

Thus far I have considered membership on the committee in large part from the demand side—that is, from the standpoint of the agents who give birth to the committee—and have examined the considerations that should come into play in forming it. But what about the supply side, the considerations in the minds of those who are asked to serve on committees?

The topic of deciding to serve or not serve on committees ought to excite the curiosity of economists and others who believe that people act to maximize their utility. Serving on committees does not seem to do that. For one thing, deciding to serve on a committee is invariably a voluntary act, and the staffer of committees is short on means—beyond persuasion—to induce people to serve. Furthermore, the rewards for serving are elusive at best. Most committee work is unpaid, and much of it is boring. Many committee activities and reports have little if any direct effect on the conduct of the organization's affairs, and committee service in the college and university setting is usually not a very effective way to advance one's academic career. Why, then, do people serve?

The answer to that question is always to be found in a mix of motives, always in different balance for any given individual, and not always accessible to the consciousness of the person who serves. Furthermore, the mix always involves some motives that can be regarded as noble, others as less noble. In reflecting on that motivational mix, I have been able to unscramble the following range of reasons why you might want to join and serve on committees.

- *Loyalty.* As colleges and universities become larger and more bureaucratized, it is often forgotten that their historical origin is of a religious character, and that, given that origin, there is a residual if weakened expectation that individuals will display a measure of unconditional loyalty to the collectivity that is the university. There is, in short, an element of the calling that survives in the academic profession, and that calling extends to serving the organization when it calls. That element of calling is symbolized in the fact that those who are asked to serve on committees are not offered and do not receive money for their services. Faculty members vary greatly in the loyalty they feel toward their home institution. It can be argued, furthermore, that in the large research university institutional loyalty has eroded as scholars fashion their careers around the attainment of prestige in academic disciplines and in national and international professional associations and groups. Nevertheless, a sufficient pool of loyalty survives so that individual faculty and staff of an institution, when asked, will serve that institution out of motives of devotion and good citizenship. The same motive exists at other levels as well: for example, in the case of the physicist who is willing to serve on otherwise unrewarding committees that appear to be useful or otherwise important to the profession.

- *Reform.* Because many committees are formed to improve an unsatisfactory state of affairs or to deal with a problem or crisis, work on such committees becomes attractive to those who believe that things can be improved by collective effort.

- *Power.* Even routine committees usually run things or report to people who run things. Problem-solving or crisis-meeting committees are often even closer to the seat of organizational power. For those who gain gratification from being near the center of things, committee service provides an opportunity. This consideration of power is tinged with ambivalence, however, because committees' power is limited; they only influence, not bind, those to whom they report. And, as often as not, committees are not very effective as political instruments. Nevertheless, there is a kind of expectation that springs eternal: By becoming involved in a collective effort—of which committee service is one form—one is endowed with power or with access to those with power, and this constitutes a motive for accepting.

- *Sociability.* While the chronic complaint is that committee life is workaday and boring, this complaint hides the fact that many of those who serve on committees find derivative gratification in interaction with colleagues and in the give-and-take of committee life. Even the shared act of complaining about service on committees is a gratifying social experience. Committee service thus can act as a kind of relief or counterbalance to the loneliness that is endemic in the highly individualized profession of academic life.

- *Psychological compensation.* In a large research university, and in many other academic institutions as well, the reward structure is such that originality in research and quality of published results constitute the principal reward for faculty members; other aspects of the academic life, such as teaching and service, play a secondary role. Regarded from another angle, research and publication tend to foster national and international reputation, while teaching and collegial service—such as committee work on the home campus—tend to foster local reputation. It is also correct to say that academics, like other people, seek their rewards where they believe they can best realize them. Taking all these observations into consideration, one can assert with some confidence that in some cases committee service comes to serve as a kind of psychological compensation for individuals who feel they do not excel in, have lost their zest for, or do not feel adequately rewarded in the world of teaching, research, and scholarly achievement. Committee service does, after all, yield rewards of the other sorts that I have listed, and a certain career gratification is gained by developing a reputation for being a good citizen. One often hears the complaint that one cannot get his or her research done on account of being tied up in too much committee work. There may be merit in this, but sometimes this complaint conceals the fact that the relationship is the other way around: People seek committee work because they cannot get the other work done to their satisfaction and gratification.

Such is the melange of motives that may induce people to undertake committee work that is otherwise not very rewarding. There is a kind of unofficial cultural value in academia that ennobles the first two sets of motives and degrades the last three. I think that is unfortunate, because, as in all other aspects of life, it is prudent not to dig too deeply into motives as long as performance is satisfactory. If that is the case, and if the motives do not lead to miscellaneous mischief, they ought to be accepted on their face as sufficient for engaging in an activity that not only is helpful but also is the source of disutility and disappointment. As for those of you who serve on committees, the main thing is to examine and come to know—insofar as that is possible—your own mix of motives when you contemplate committee service. Not all of these may be the most noble, but if you are aware of them, this reduces the likelihood of regretting in the future that you have either missed an opportunity or wasted your time.

3 | Inside the Black Box

Almost everything I have written up to this point is about the committee in an organizational context: its functions in that context, its types, and the organizational circumstances of its formation. At this point I turn to the committee work itself—or, better, the committee at work. I address this topic from three angles: (a) from the standpoint of committee as small-group process (this chapter), (b) from the standpoint of the serving member (Chapter 4), and (c) from the standpoint of the chair (Chapter 5).

As a social group, the committee invariably falls into that category we call *instrumental*. It is formed to get some kind of work done; it usually works according to a deadline for finishing that work; and it usually delivers a product in the form of a discrete set of decisions (for example, admitting students, recommending appointments) or in the shape of a formal report. Such a report contains a mixture of facts, diagnoses and analyses, statements of priorities, recommendations, and a defense of those recommendations. As an instrumental group, it differs from other groups that we call *expressive*—street corner gangs, families at dinner, conversational groups at a party, groups of people watching a sports event on television.

The distinction between instrumental and expressive groups is a helpful one, but should not be regarded as too fixed. Any given group reveals both aspects and can switch from one type to another. If a family at dinner begins to discuss where it should take its vacation next summer or whether to buy a car, it turns in an instrumental direction. If a board of trustees or a committee falls into joking or teasing, or breaks for coffee, it has changed in an expressive direction. Furthermore, even as a committee proceeds seriously with its work, an expressive aspect is always at work: People are enjoying or not enjoying themselves; hostility is being expressed and answered; and moods of collective anxiety, depression, satisfaction, and elation are continuously ebbing and flowing. The elements of instrumental and expressive, then, should best be understood as ever-present and important *aspects* of groups.

The Instrumental Side of Committee Life

Back in the 1950s, a group of scholars at Harvard University, led by Robert Freed Bales, carried out an extensive range of experiments on instrumental small groups.[1] Constituted of Harvard students, these groups were asked by the experimenter in their sessions to come up with a suggested solution for some sort of problem—for example, how to resolve a conflict in an office situation. These groups could therefore be regarded as committees in miniature. Each group met on a periodic basis, and the behavior of the members in the meetings was recorded in great detail through a one-way mirror and subsequently analyzed.

Not all the groups studied were able to come up with solutions; these could be regarded as aborted instrumental groups. But those that did produce solutions (equivalent to committee reports) seemed to go through certain phases during the course of their meetings:

- During the early meetings the behavior of the group members appeared to focus above all on the discovery and establishment of *facts* that were relevant to the problem that had been set for them: How did the conflict begin? What issues appeared to be at stake? Who seemed to start the conflict? Who appeared to have suffered losses in the conflict? and so on.

- Also in the early meetings there was a lot of discussion of the *rights and wrongs* of the conflict situation and the assignment of responsibility.

- As the meetings progressed, interest tended to focus less on the facts of the case, and members began to come up with *suggested solutions or lines of action* about ways to resolve the conflict. These were aired, discussed, modified, elaborated, and sometimes discarded.

- As the group moved into its final phases, activity focused on the *commitment to a definite decision,* which was conveyed to the experimenter as a product of the group's work.

Two other features of these experiments should be mentioned. First, there was a sort of internal logic to the several phases that Bales and his coresearchers discovered. If, for example, some member of the group "jumped the gun" and began proposing solutions at a very early moment in the group meetings, these suggestions were invariably rejected, often with a some hostility directed toward the proposer. It was as though such suggestions were premature, and there had to be a period of gathering, sifting, selecting, and evaluating facts before it was appropriate for decisions to be considered or made. This process occurred more or less unconsciously, in the sense that the groups themselves did not monitor or comment on what was going on in the group.

Second, as the group sessions went along, a certain *division of labor* among group members often developed. Certain individuals would appear to be more active with respect to establishing the facts, while others would take the lead in suggesting lines of action (and would thus become "leaders" in directing the group's work). Some would talk a great deal, others scarcely at all. Some would concentrate on asking questions, others on supplying answers and giving directions. In short, a group structure began to emerge, with different "types" of committee members—idea persons, action persons, actives, passives—and with clear patterns of leadership and followership.

Although the sequences of behavior identified in the Bales experiments were only general patterns and did not apply perfectly to any one group, the analogies between these groups and formal committees are apparent. Like these small groups, committees are assigned to undertake some kind of task that is understood tacitly through the known purpose of the committee or is specified in its formal charge. At its moment of birth, the committee is assigned a very minimal structure: a "chair" with only general expectations about his or her role and a discreet number of "members" who are all equal to one another in the sense that none is given any functionally specified task but is asked only to be a responsible participant. In short, the committee, by omission, is asked to evolve its own structure.

Above all, a committee is asked to come up with some kind of decision or suggestion for decision ("recommendations"); it is asked to engage in investigation and argumentation. This means that a committee, if its work is complete, will have to touch several bases that are essential for developing an argument. The most important of these are the following:

identifying and agreeing upon what *facts* are relevant to its work —this is the investigatory aspect of committee work;

determining why certain facts are relevant to its work and others are not; this is what is being done when statements such as "that's not relevant" or "that's not important" are heard in committee meetings—the criteria of relevance are to be found in the broader *context* of the committee's work—its explicit and implicit charge, and its own building definition of its mission;

diagnosing selected patterns of facts and determining why they are problematical—to explain why an array of facts constitutes a *problem* calling for action;

considering *lines of action* that will reduce the problematical status of the situation diagnosed—this is the consideration of recommendations proper;

selecting among the different lines of action and developing *priorities and preferences* among them;

defending and giving *legitimacy* to the selected recommendation; this may have several ingredients: (a) showing that the recommendations are *consistent* with the facts, assessments of facts, and problem identified; (b) invoking *normative standards* to justify the preferences and recommendations advanced—standards such as efficiency or equity; (c) if necessary, appealing to certain common *values* to justify the normative standards invoked.

This list is meant to account for the content of much of what goes on in committee work. In routine, decision-making committees, almost all these elements are taken for granted, and the committee may move easily from facts to decisions and recommendations if the other elements are tacitly understood and agreed-upon. In other cases all of the elements are present. To take a single illustration of this, Box 3.1 shows the "anatomy" of a committee recommendation.

The list in the box not only indicates what committees *accomplish* in carrying out their assigned tasks of investigation, argumentation, and recommendation, but also identifies the nodal points of *disagreement, conflict,* and *failure* in committee deliberations. For example, in the blue-ribbon committee we argued about the authenticity of facts and the validity of claims that came before us; we argued at length and repeatedly as to whether the suggested merger of the athletics programs would achieve any real economies, and the committee report, which claimed that it could, was criticized for claiming that. We argued repeatedly as to whether the unification of men's and women's sports would constitute a disadvantage or advantage for women in terms of distribution of resources and facilities to them and their representation in the decision-making apparatus. We could have argued about

Box 3.1

The Anatomy of a Committee Recommendation: Merging the Athletic Programs at Berkeley

1. The committee determined certain historical facts about why men's athletics, women's athletics, and recreational sports had been separated from one another in the first place: For example, women's and men's athletics had been separated because women were not then competing in NCAA (National Collegiate Athletic Association) sports, and there was reluctance to treat them in the same way as those (men's) sports that were. The committee also described the facts of the existing administrative arrangements— separate directors and separate ancillary services (e.g., ticket sales) attached to each—as well as the level of resources available to each, and the long history of struggle among them for these resources.

2. The committee tacitly justified the selection of these facts by reference to the demands in the charge that we attend to budgetary issues and issues of administrative reporting —that is, that they were "relevant" to the charge.

3. The committee pointed out that the troika-like arrangement of the directorships (each group of sports had a separate athletic director) and divisions seemed to be duplicative and wasteful of resources, administratively messy, and productive of difficult-to-control conflict. The committee observed that all three divisions seemed to be chronically dissatisfied with their share of the resources available for athletics. These observations permitted the committee to characterize the existing situation as "problematical."

the validity of bringing the value premises of economy, equity, and administrative rationality to bear; but we did not because they were matters of consensus and were never challenged.

4. The committee laid out a series of options, including maintaining the status quo, for the administrative structures and reporting relationships of the three branches of athletics.

5. The committee ultimately called for a complete administrative merger of the three branches under one athletic director, with coaches of both men's and women's teams, and coaches of recreational sports reporting to the athletic director or an associate director.

6. The committee pointed out that the envisioned recommendation would likely achieve some economies (by unifying promotion, ticket sales, public relations, etc., into one agency rather than having separate agencies for each), would be administratively neater, and would constitute a structural arrangement likely to reduce conflict. The committee also considered certain objections to the merger, especially the apprehension on the part of representatives of women's sports that women wold be disadvantaged through absorption, and suggested safeguards against this effect. Finally, the committee did not mention explicitly but made known through argumentation that the value premises that guided our recommendations were those of economy and efficiency, equity among different sports, administrative rationality, and maximizing peace and harmony.

The Expressive Side of Committee Life

The term *expressive* refers to the fact that a group—in our case, a committee—has to spend part of its energy in safeguarding its own integrity. A committee must have rules or understandings about who talks when, when it gets into a state of unfocused discourse, when and how it comes to decisions, and how it affirms those decisions (e.g., by informal consensus; by majority vote). More generally, groups—including committees—are forever in danger of bogging down in their work through lack of direction, frustration, loss of interest, low morale, alienation of members, and internal conflict. Many groups do break down and fail in their work for these "expressive" reasons, and those that do not have to devote some of their time and energy—sometimes consciously, sometimes unconsciously—to seeing that they do not.

Most committees, especially when they are small, proceed with a minimum of procedural rules. A committee of three or five that is arranging the details of a graduation ceremony, for example, does not need many rules beyond those understandings of conversational civility—understandings about not talking too much or too little, not shouting or insulting, not interrupting incessantly, and so on. It is only in moments of excited talk or conflict that the chair will have to make explicit the familiar rule that people will talk in the order that he or she recognizes them. Small, informal committees of this sort also do not need elaborate procedures for coming to decisions. Decisions may be made when someone asks, "Are we agreed that . . . " or suggests "Let's decide that . . ." and assent is given.

As groups grow larger, more formal procedures come into play. If 12 to 15 people are discussing whether a statistics requirement ought to be included in an undergraduate social-science major, almost everybody will have something to say and disagreements of educational philosophy and pedagogical strategy will inevitably arise. At the very least the chair of such a group has to maintain order by recognizing or people in order, setting limits on how long a given topic should be discussed, and guiding the discussion to some kind of conclusion, even if that conclusion should be deciding not to decide.

The most formal expression of procedural order for meetings, including committee meetings, is found in books such as *Robert's Rules of Order*. These are extremely complex documents that specify, for example, when the chair of a group may silence someone ("You are out of order"), when someone can interrupt without being recognized ("Point of order!"), when things can and cannot be discussed (for example, if an amendment is made to a motion, the amendment must be discussed before the motion is discussed), and how meetings begin ("calling to order") and end ("rules of adjournment"). Books of this sort are akin to rule books for games like baseball. They aim to specify *every* possible situational contingency that may arise in a game or a meeting and to specify a corresponding rule that covers it. Rules of order, like rules of the game, are designed to minimize uncertainty and ambiguity. Such an objective can never be fully attained, of course. Baseball games need umpires to make calls and invoke rules, and deliberative bodies need chairs and sometimes parliamentarians to decide what kind of situation is at hand and what rules apply. Both games and meetings thus have a residue of judgment and arbitrariness, but the rules of order attempt to minimize these and even contain procedures for reducing arbitrariness (for example, appealing an umpire's decision to the league office; overruling a chair's decision).

Many committees, then, are shrouded in rules and procedures. However, it might be suggested that if a chair, a parliamentarian, or a member of a deliberative group is forced to consult the rule book, it is a sign that the group is in trouble. To invoke a rule is often a sign that informal civility has broken down.

When groups work themselves into a paralysis through *procedural* or parliamentary wrangling, that signifies, to me at least, that they are probably paralyzed by substantive conflict. Prolonged procedural discussions often mean that groups are either finding refuge in elaborate procedural discussions as a way of working their way out of the thickets of conflict or that some people in the group are attempting to score *substantive* victories by prevailing on procedural points. Elaborate rules of order serve best when they are an unused reservoir. By that I mean that the committees that work best are those that rely on informal understandings of civility and cooperativeness, move toward consensus in easy ways, and settle issues and decisions without actually invoking rules and voting.

In addition to sustaining itself procedurally, the committee confronts other contingencies that are expressive in the more literal sense of that term—that is, the complications that arise from people expressing themselves. In my committee experience, I have identified a whole range of often-subtle emotional aspects of committee life that counter the common view that committee work is dry, affectless, and, above all, joyless. Among the most salient of these affect-laden aspects are the following:

• *Initial posturing.* A committee meeting together for the first time often has two conspicuous features. First, the committee members do not know one another very well. This is not true for a departmental committee of colleagues, but it may well be true for a campuswide committee and is certainly true of a national committee with representatives from diverse institutions and regions. This means that, for any given member, the other committee members constitute a new audience. Second, many committees—especially those that are regarded as "important" or "blue ribbon"—will have important people, including narcissists and prima donnas, as members.

Because of these two features, the first sessions of a committee's existence are likely to be marked by the putting forth of pet ideas, the floating of dazzling insights, the displaying of unusual knowledge, the dropping of names and places—in short, the making of partially disguised statements about one's personal importance for the sake of the audience. This seems an inevitable dynamic of committee life and should be recognized as such. I have witnessed chairs who acknowledge this dynamic by asking every member, in the early phases of a committee's work, to say what he or she believes to be the single most important issue before the committee. I also heard a *rapporteur* of a meeting, when asked to summarize its proceedings, remark wryly, "The best summary I can give is that everybody here said what they came to say." The more serious aspects of posturing are that it may prove to be disruptive because it upstages and may provoke defensive or aggressive behavior on the part of other members, thus starting the committee off on a competitive note.

- *Inclusion and solidarity.* At the beginning of a committee's work the chair will typically go around the room and ask each member to identify and say a few words about him- or herself. (This operation may indeed be a gentle, informal invitation for people to posture—including posturing by saying almost nothing about themselves, thereby suggesting that all that should be known about them is already known.) The evident value of this exercise is to familiarize unknown people with one another, but it is also a ritual gesture of inclusion and solidarity. More generally, part of the "civility" of committee meetings is the recurrence of respectful phrases such as "I understand your point . . . ," "The strongest part of your argument is . . . ," and the inevitable compliment that precedes a "but" when the speaker's actual intent is to disagree. Furthermore, as we will see later, one rule of thumb for the successful chair is that he or she ensure that, to the greatest degree possible, every member of the committee feels included in some way in the collective project. All these items deal with the familiar phenomenon of group cohesion, which lies at the heart of group morale.

- *Friendships and cliques.* Part of the phenomenon of solidarity in committee work is the development of subsolidarities among small groups of committee members. Some committee members who arrive on the scene may be friends already. In addition, members quickly develop affinities with others in the course of committee work, as they hear expressions of opinion similar to their own, as they are impressed with the insightfulness or brilliance of a comment, or as they experience the presence of a soul-mate. At one level the development of these subsolidarities constitutes a positive asset for the committee as a whole, because it diminishes people's feelings that they are being excluded. On the other hand, if the subsolidarities develop into some kind of clique with a solidified position on many issues— in short, if they become a bloc—this constitutes a source of rigidity within the committee. This in turn may contribute to its polarization into contending subgroups, which works at cross-purposes with the development of solidarity in the group as a whole.

- *Stereotyping and scapegoating.* One manifestation of group cohesion is that its members come to have a feeling of like-mindedness about one another, even though they may come to disagree on specific points. As indicated, this is a positive asset for committee work. At the same time, like-mindedness also generates a kind of continuous surveillance of the scene for people who seem not to be like-minded (i.e., who deviate from group expectations), and to assume a punitive posture to those identified as such. The first process is called *stereotyping*, the second *scapegoating*. Committees often endow one or more committee members with labels such as "Mr. Agreeable," "troublemaker," "stickler," "nervous nellie," "motormouth," or some other negative tab. Almost as if to facilitate this process, some people seem to assume behavioral postures that invite stereotyping; it is as though they enjoy being typecast. In any event, those so labeled then become the butt of teasing, unkind jokes, and sometimes outright cruelty. I have observed many instances when committee members join together and invite the chair to call down or otherwise punish a scapegoated member.

Stereotyping and scapegoating cut two ways. On the one hand, they simultaneously reflect and reinforce group solidarity and in this way contribute to group morale. On the other, the processes are usually not pleasant for those so treated, and may ultimately lead directly or indirectly to disruptive behavior on their part. Moreover, when the chair becomes the object of stereotyping and scapegoating (as stupid, passive, domineering, or whatever), this often sets the stage for committee crisis and failure, because his or her leadership is effectively undermined.

- *Idealization.* This is the flip side of scapegoating. It involves the singling out of leaders in committee—sometimes, but not necessarily the chair—for positive stereotyping as the smartest, as the most helpful, as the best citizen, as the hardest worker (the hardest worker may be negatively stereotyped as the "eager beaver," too), or, indeed, as the leader of the scapegoaters. Such idealization is always fraught with ambivalence, however, and is correspondingly frail. Just as the scapegoat may be forgiven and brought back into good standing, so may the group hero, with one false move, fall from grace and be victimized through the hostility that accompanies disillusionment.

- *Tension release and humor.* In the Bales experiments with small groups, the investigators often discovered a final phase—occurring even after the agreement on a final group disposition and line of action—in which there was flurry of affective behavior, such as hostile comments, joking, laughing, and good fellowship. (This final phase is also frequently marked by ritual expressions of solidarity—for example, vows on the part of committee members to look one another up later, even when it is tacitly known that this will not happen.) All of us who have served on committees have witnessed these final expressive episodes. They are often made more or less explicit in the form of a celebration dinner or party at the home of the chair or another committee member. The dynamics behind the final expression of tension are several. First, the processes of cohesion, stereotyping, scapegoating, and idealization inevitably tap a reservoir of unresolved affects that are permitted expression only at the moment when the committee is dissolving and will, in all likelihood, never meet again. Second, the taking of decisive action at the end a committee's work inevitably implies that some committee members have got their way and others have not, that there is a majority and a minority, that there are the victors and the vanquished. As a result, residual feelings of both pride and humiliation remain. The expressions of hostility (for example, "roasting") and the celebrative moods that appear at the end of a committee's work seem to be largely unconscious ways of dealing with these accumulated affects.

- *The need for a happy ending.* This idea encapsulates the dynamics of the final, expressive phase of committee work. The journey is at an end, and, as a rule, people like to leave with good feelings about it. This lies behind the often unconscious dread of one or more "minority reports" accompanying the major committee report, because it symbolizes that hard feelings have not been resolved and that the group has not achieved that mythic state of happy cohesion at the end.

There are two psychodynamic reasons why all these affective sides constitute subterranean but real aspects of committee life. The first is that *any* social group, including the most impersonal committee, takes on some of the characteristics of the most primitive social group of all—the family—if for no other reason than that the members bring their own family histories and their derived affects to the group. It is inevitable, for example, that diffuse feelings of authority will be excited by a committee, because at the very least a committee is always constituted with a simple system of authority—the chair with some authority over members. Indeed, and ironically, the committee approximates classical group depicted by Freud in his *Group Psychology and the Analysis of the Ego*: a group with one leader who is distinguished by his equal elevation over all others and a body of members who are equal in their subservience, and who seek inclusion, affection, and distributive justice from that leader. (This is not to claim that all committees are reproductions of Freud's primary group, but it is to say that the committee, with group characteristics, always excites generalized and diffuse affects.) In addition, committees may be expected to manifest, albeit in disguised form, the whole affective gamut of rivalry, jealousy, destructiveness, anxiety, affection, and elation associated originally with the family and ultimately with all group life.

Second, the committee is a creature with a temporally finite existence. It is born, it enjoys a life, and it dies. In that respect work on a committee may be said to resemble a kind of ocean voyage or odyssey, in which people are brought or thrown together for an experience, but with the full knowledge that the experience will end. So, in the expressive side of its existence, the committee excites—in a subterranean way, at least—all the feelings of union and dissolution that are associated with the human experience of life and death generally, as well as the accompanying feelings of separation and anxiety, loss and sadness, reminiscence and nostalgia, euphoria and despair. No life experience transpires without these deeper human feelings, and even the most superficial or boring experience in committee life excites them at least minimally.

This account of the instrumental and expressive aspects of committee life also confirms the fact that committee life involves a subtle division of roles and "committee types" that may correspond to those aspects. The least interesting of these roles are the formal ones that arise out of the instrumental purposes of the committee's life—chair, vice chair, recorder, subcommittee chair, subcommittee member, and so on. They are uninteresting because they are explicit, consciously acknowledged, and routine. The more interesting roles are the informal ones that give spice to committee life: the hero, the villain, the scapegoat, the clown, the jokester, the benign, the obnoxious—in short, the good and the evil. There is no single, definitive list of committee roles and types, but one further aspect of Bales's work on group dynamics may be mentioned. In many of those groups that were "successful" by Bales's measures—that is, those that produced results, felt good about their work, and did not break apart— an interesting *coalition* emerged. This was the coalition between a person identified as the "instrumental leader" (who moved the group along toward its goal, mobilized others, and kept control) and the "expressive leader" (who showed interest in, joked with, and became friendly with the other group members, and who was generally the "best liked"). By "coalition" Bales meant that the instrumental leader and the expressive leader liked one another and communicated a great deal with one another. Bales went so far as to liken the coalition of instrumental and expressive leaders in groups to the coalition between father and mother in a family—with the other members as children—but in my estimation that carried speculation a bit far. The finding did indicate, however, that when there is systematic though unconscious attention to the instrumental and expressive aspects of group life, and when these two kinds of attention are linked with one another, the prognosis for effective group functioning is good.

The Evolution of a Committee Culture

Through the dynamics I have identified in this chapter, every committee experiences the development of a "committee culture"—or had better do so if it is going to work together.

How does this culture develop? It involves first of all the building of a committee memory. People are continuously remembering things that were said and points that were made in past meetings, and identifying those things with other committee members. It involves some benign and some not-so-benign stereotyping. Members come to assume roles in committees by taking a particular line, and these roles are solidified by typing them, by labeling them, by joking about them. Other, scapegoated members come to symbolize what the committee culture does not stand for: incivility, disagree-ableness, stubbornness, and the like. The committee culture is also built through the development of rules and under-standings about how to proceed: some from the book, some imported from members' experience on other committees, some generated through the give-and-take of the commit-tee's own work.

Through all this there develops a sense of the committee as a definite entity set off from the rest of the world at least temporarily, which is also an essential aspect of a culture. And finally, there develops a feeling on the part of committee mem-bers that they are somehow special, even though this "spe-cialness" may be experienced in a modest way. And, having developed this committee culture, committees proceed fur-ther to develop a their own little world of rituals, "in jokes," and immodest self-congratulation, as well as an implicit and sometimes explicit hostility to outsiders who are not part of the culture. All this is to say that a committee is no different from any other type of group, and if a committee is to main-tain any integrity and any capacity to function, it must nec-essarily develop a common culture of which its members feel they are a part.

Note

1. The best references for this work are to be found in Robert F. Bales, *Interaction Process Analysis: A Method for the Study of Small Groups* (Cam-bridge, MA: Addison-Wesley, 1950); Robert F. Bales, "The Equilibrium Problem in Small Groups," in Talcott Parsons, Robert F. Bales, and Edward

A. Shils, *Working Papers in the Theory of Action* (Glencoe, IL: Free Press, 1953), pp. 111-161; and Robert F. Bales and Philip E. Slater, "Role Differentiation in Small Decision-Making Groups," in Talcott Parsons and Robert F. Bales (in collaboration with James Olds, Morris Zelditch, Jr., and Philip E. Slater), *Family, Socialization, and Interaction Process* (Glencoe, IL: Free Press, 1955), pp. 259-306.

4 | How to Serve

I remember my first committee assignment as an experience filled with dread. As a young faculty member of 28, I was asked to serve on the Committee on Economic Growth of the Social Science Research Council, which met mainly in New York. Everybody on the committee was much my senior; the committee included such "heavies" as Simon Kuznets, Joseph Spengler, Bert Hoselitz, Melville Herskovits, and Wilbert Moore. At my first meeting the committee simply moved on without particularly noticing my presence beyond introducing me around. The assumption was that I would enter running, whereas in reality I entered nervously feeling my way. Furthermore, there was no feedback beyond the one-sentence remark of Wilbert Moore, who sponsored my membership, that Kuznets, the chair, thought I was "all right."

I do not think my experience on that committee was all that unusual. Learning on committees is done almost entirely by doing, and seldom is one told how he or she is doing. It is something like college or university teaching; there is a tacit assumption that simply because one has gained a higher degree, he or she knows how to teach. (Box 4.1, however, lists 10 "rules" for participation; these points will guide this chapter's discussion.)

Box 4.1

Ten Rules for Serving on Committees

1. Know your assignment.
2. Know when you are being co-opted.
3. Know how to represent your constituencies.
4. Time your interventions.
5. Keep your comments in context.
6. Follow through on your contributions.
7. Do not attack other committee members.
8. Rely on humor.
9. Avoid extremes and scapegoating yourself.
10. Do not follow these rules to the point of becoming a phony.

One does learn, however, even though much of the learning is unconscious and never articulated. Even a very experienced committee member believes that he or she is simply "being oneself" on a committee and does not think, much less plot, very much in terms of strategies and tactics. For this reason, the following abstracted rules of thumb for behaving as a committee member are just that: abstracted from many years of experience and reflection, not carried around in my head as so many strategies every time I go into a committee meeting. That being said, let me specify several principles that seem to foster effectiveness and influence in committee work.

Knowing Your Assignment

This information can usually be gained by asking the person who asks you to join or by asking others who have served on that or similar committees. I have made at least three mistakes along these lines in my committee life. The first two stemmed from my not finding out how boring was the committee work on the Committee on Educational Policy and the Committee on Committees of Berkeley's Academic Senate. I accepted the chair of the first while I was abroad, and I accepted the invitation to put my name on the ballot for the second (it was an elected committee), because a group of my friends convinced me how politically important it was for me to be on that committee. The third mistake was accepting an appointment to the nominations committee of the International Sociological Association at its IX World Congress (1978) in Uppsala under the false belief that I would have some effect on the nominations of candidates for office of that association. As it turned out, almost every decision on that score had been already made, and there was nothing to do but to accept the inevitable or resign from the committee. The latter did not seem a very productive line of action, because it would have done little good for me or anybody else at the time.

Knowing When You Are Being Co-opted

In many cases the issue of co-optation does not arise, because the committee itself is not a controversial one or because you do not feel all that strongly about the issues before it. Sometimes, however, you may feel that you are being asked to join a politically meaningful committee because you represent a constituency or a point of view. If that is so, you must decide (a) not to join, if it compromises your point of view, because joining usually means compromising; (b) to join with an eye to representing your point of view but accepting the need to compromise; or (c) to join in order to fight for your position but risk marginalization on the committee by doing so. None of these three alternatives is the "right" one, but you should understand what you are getting yourself in for.

Knowing How to Represent Your Constituencies

Once having decided to join, the issue remains as to how much you want to represent your constituency or interests and how much you want to become a part of a cooperative "committee culture." Resolving this does not always involve a conscious, deliberate decision, but it is always an issue. On any committee you always potentially represent some constituency whether you wish to or not. I cannot deny that I am a sociologist at an interdisciplinary social-science conference. I cannot deny that I am an American sociologist in the context of the International Sociological Association. I cannot deny that I am from the Berkeley campus in a universitywide committee meeting. I cannot deny that I am a senior rather than a junior faculty member. And I cannot deny that I am one of those who has a liberal rather than a radical view of university politics when I serve on a committee dealing with campus matters.

The principal question, then, is not *whether* you represent constituencies but *how* you represent them. I have found that to represent your own constituency militantly or even explicitly is not effective, as a rule, for two reasons. First and mainly, you suffer a loss of credibility as your statements are likely to be read as expressions of personal interest. For example, the Committee on Basic Research in the Behavioral and Social Sciences was made up of representatives of about eight disciplines. At one stage of our work we were planning the contents of a volume that would present leading edges of research in all the relevant disciplines. One committee member, a physiological psychologist, insisted early, hotly, and repeatedly that research in his particular subdiscipline was so vital and important that at least one third of the entire report should be dedicated to it. This member was branded as a kind of self-interested hog by the remainder of the committee, and he thereby lost a good deal of effectiveness and influence. Along the same lines, I have always observed in systemwide committee meetings of the University of California that if my colleagues from Berkeley announce that Berkeley cannot tolerate a certain policy or practice, the main effect of that kind of assertion is to excite and consolidate anti-Berkeley sentiments on the part of other committee members.

Second, insistent representation of your own constituency and its point of view is likely to be counterproductive because it disrupts the development of the culture of the committee. As I argued before, a committee culture implies that the group develops a sense of its own collective identity and specialness and that members show some loyalty to that sense. Representation of self-interest is disruptive to that process, even though members of the committee may not recognize or describe that effect in precisely those terms.

The best strategy, then, appears to represent your constituents' interests—you must do so if you believe in standing up for your constituents—but to do so in terms that are as disarming, general, and couched in language other than self-interest as possible. I say this with no cynical intent and with no intent to encourage dishonesty or dissimulation, but in the spirit of maximizing your effectiveness and influence in the committee setting while at the same time implicitly acknowledging the committee dynamics that are at work.

Timing Your Interventions

I have witnessed countless occasions in committee meetings when a member who introduces a definite proposal very early in the proceedings sees it derailed or defeated. To illustrate, when my Committee on Basic Research in the Behavioral and Social Sciences was exploring, rather leisurely, areas in which exciting new social-scientific research was likely to be done in the coming decade, one of the members present—a very eminent and respected social scientist—leaped in energetically and argued with some heat that the subject of "social scientists as expert witnesses" was such an area and ought to be included. Subsequent discussion evoked one critical remark after another that picked away at this suggestion, but the proposer never relented. When the proposal was finally shot down, the proposer withdrew from participation in something of a huff. I have sometimes thought that if he had bided his time and introduced his suggestion more quietly at a later time, and couched it in terms that avoided types of criticisms that had already been made of *other* proposals, his chances of success would have been much improved.

Along the same lines, it is safe to say that it is much more self-defeating to talk too much than to talk too little in committees. Of course, to say nothing leaves you completely without influence, unless you bend your efforts to influencing other committee members outside meeting times. But giving long-winded speeches or lectures is a sure avenue to creating disgruntlement and making yourself a scapegoat. It generates murmurs during coffee breaks about people who like to hear themselves talk and not-so-subtle suggestions to the chair to "do something about X." In a way this is a curious point to make, because most academics like to talk; but perhaps it is for that very reason that they do not like to hear others talk at length, no matter how intelligent they might sound.

Keeping Your Comments in Context

The value of a well-timed, synthetic intervention that takes into account the context of what has been said in the prior discussion is the kind of contribution to committee work that is likely to have maximum impact. For one thing, such an intervention can be phrased in such a way as to take account of what others have said, thus incorporating their points directly or indirectly, which is, in turn, a way of gaining their support. For another, such an intervention is unlikely to be considered as coming "from left field" and thus regarded as irresponsible or out of keeping with the progress of the committee's work. The only risk involved in this kind of synthetic proposal is that you run the risk of usurping the chair's authority, because an implicit code of committee work is that it is usually the chair's task to seek for points of articulation and consensus. I will say more on this topic in the next two chapters.

Following Through on Your Contributions

Once you have made a point or stated a position that seems to gain favor or consensus, it is important to see that it does not get lost. The best way of doing this, moreover, is unobtrusively to volunteer to write down "some language" that might prove "helpful" as preliminary draft material to the committee and the chair in discussing the point further. I recall after a long discussion on the nature of the different social-science disciplines that transpired in our Committee on Basic Research in the Behavioral and Social Sciences, I remarked that I had been doing some independent thinking about this matter and would be willing to write down my thoughts for the committee's consideration at a future meeting. That draft subsequently became the basis for one of the main chapters in the final report.

In volunteering to follow through in this way, you take on the role of "drafter," which, as we will see later, is among the most important and powerful roles in committee work. Again, there is some danger that volunteering to draft will be seen as usurping the chair's responsibility. But if the volunteering is done modestly, after consulting the chair, and in a spirit of helpfulness, that risk is small.

Not Attacking Other Committee Members

I know there are differences of opinion on this point, but as a general rule it is wise to avoid the direct expression of hostility in committees. Expressing one's own sense of outrage at an idea or a person is hard to control, and it is always tempting to be drawn into the scapegoating process in the committee setting. On some occasions, moreover, the act of "blowing up" can break some sort of logjam or move the committee to act. In general, though, expressing hostility costs more in terms of problems created than it does in promoting committee effectiveness or influencing the course of events in the direction you desire. For one thing, expressing hostility invites revenge—if not immediately, then somewhere down the line. It also constitutes a kind of open invitation for other committee members to rally around the person who has been attacked. But most of all, an angry attack usually constitutes an affront to expectations of civility that are a part of committee culture, and it conveys to other committee members that you are out of control, which you ought not to be, according to the standards of that culture.

Relying on Humor

The advantages of timely use of humor in a committee cannot be exaggerated. It is difficult to speak of guidelines in this respect, because a person's sense of humor is a kind of "given" and one cannot be coached into having one. Notwithstanding, its advantages are numerous. To reveal a sense of humor is a way of communicating that one maintains a certain distance from the proceedings, and it implies that one has neither defensive nor aggrandizing intent. Humor also constitutes a way of attacking an idea or another person without being openly discrediting.

I can recall one incident at a meeting of a committee of the systemwide Academic Senate when we were discussing, somewhat wearily, the subject of "mandatory matriculation," an arcane aspect of transferring from community colleges to the University of California. Almost nobody understood or was interested in the subject, and nobody seemed to know what we were supposed to do about it. At a given moment, I observed, quite spontaneously, that "mandatory matricula-tion" sounded to me like an obscure form of sexual malfunc-tioning. Though I had not consciously intended the remark to have this effect, it brought forward loud laughter and effectively killed the discussion—which, I might add mod-estly, was well on its way to dying a natural death, anyway. Humor, finally, is a way of simultaneously expressing hos-tility, releasing tension, and, oddly, becoming the object of other members' affection. I cannot say that I understand the dy-namics of this, but I have often found myself and seen others being drawn to the committee wag who knows how and when to joke in good taste, how to attack without seeming to attack, and how to expose without revealing an intention to expose. I have also experienced this effect when I have taken on that role.

Avoiding Extremes and Self-Scapegoating

I do not know how to make the last point without seeming banal, but it is so important that it must be mentioned. It has to do with avoiding all kinds of extremes in committee work. The effective committee member must talk but not become verbose, be humorous but not biting, be serious but not funereal, be conscientious but not compulsive, be knowl-edgeable but not arrogant, be prepared to defend what he or she has said without being defensive, be cooperative but not submissive, and be a good citizen without overconforming. If one attacks another point of view or argument that one finds stupid or otherwise unacceptable, it ought to be done carefully, in a measured way, and in the context of venturing other comments that grant *general* legitimacy to the person being attacked.

These several "golden mean" observations add up to the truth that moderation and tact are two of the most valuable assets in the committee setting. There are a couple of reasons for this. First, these characteristics are normally highly valued in the code of civility that constitutes the committee culture. Second, if one moves toward any extremes of behavior in this kind of group setting, one invites being typecast and even scapegoated. (Actually, the tactful committee member *also* runs the risk of being Mr. or Ms. Moderate if he or she is caricatured in the expression of moderation.) And if typecast or scapegoated, the committee member then runs the risk of losing flexibility and influence, because his or her conduct is discounted as showing predictability.

So much for a set of guidelines that have proven helpful in committee work over the years. I think they have some general validity in the committee context. I should end with a final bit of qualifying advice: *Do not follow these rules to the point of becoming a phony.* Insofar as what I have outlined involves the expression of a personal style of my own, you should discount that appropriately, because your personal style is your own and difficult to alter. If you consciously attempt to alter it, moreover, you are likely to be seen for what you are: unauthentic. And the quality of unauthenticity is certainly not an asset in the committee setting.

5 | How to Chair

The perfect committee chair, like the perfect academic administrator, is one of those "walk-on-water" creatures that never exists in reality. If you are an ideal chair, you must possess an unattainable balance of personal qualities. You can be neither passive nor dictatorial, but, ideally, should mix these qualities in a style of noncoercive, open authoritativeness. You should be able to relate with civility to all constituencies within and outside the committee, whether they be agreeable or disagreeable. You should have political sensitivity and tact, but at the same time have a forceful command of the spoken and written language. Because of these semicontradictory demands on a chair, it is difficult to generate consistent advice about the optimum chairlike behavior. Yet some helpful rules of thumb can be elucidated (see Box 5.1).

As formal roles go, that of the chair has qualities of vagueness and flexibility. Those qualities are seen in the variable amount of power institutionalized in the role. In some cases the position is an extremely weak one. At the London School of Economics, for example, the chair is called the *convener*, a term that suggests that his or her sole power is to determine when meetings will be held. Most chairs in academic departments in arts and science in the United States are also quite weak, last for shorter periods (3 years is typical) and involve

---

Box 5.1

Ten Rules for Chairing Committees

1. Know the limits of and demands on your assignment.
2. Know the purpose(s) of the committee.
3. Know what resources to expect.
4. Know the size and composition of your committee.
5. Negotiate before rather than after accepting the chair.
6. Respond to the collective task at hand.
7. Keep the business moving, but do not rush it.
8. Be open and accommodating.
9. Deal with conflict head-on.
10. Stay on top of terminal tensions.

---

brokering between colleagues and higher administration as their main function. As a result, deans and provosts typically find a high level of unwillingness to serve among faculty members. Many Canadian counterparts are called "heads," serve for terms up to 10 years, and have a greater range of authority. Chairs of departments in medical schools are granted even more power. Another source of vagueness in the role of chair is that, no matter what the level of instituted authority, the expectations as to *style* of administering (passive, easy-going, hard-driving, meticulous, dictatorial) are generally left unspoken and up to the dispositions and predilections of the individual incumbents.

The role of chair of a committee is also an open one. In the case of routine, processing committees (such as a graduate admissions committee or a course committee of a college), it is seldom expected that a chair be much more than hard-working and congenial with his or her colleagues, because there are so few contingencies involved in the working life of the committee. Even when one is asked to chair a major committee to investigate, diagnose, and recommend in an area of trouble, little more than the invitation to chair—"Can I persuade you to chair the X committee?"—is typically extended. The role of chair is well enough known, however, so that question implies spending the necessary, open-ended amount of time in the coming months; scheduling meetings, "chairing" those meetings in the sense of setting agendas, covering topics, guiding discussions, and keeping order; forming subcommittees if necessary; and being responsible for writing or coordinating the writing of the mandated report, which is the ultimate committee product.

In the case of invitations to chair routine committees, the invitee seldom needs to ask questions; the duties of the committee are well known, and the main question that usually occupies the mind of the invitee is whether he or she is willing to spend the time to do the job. In the case of the major one-time committee, the person invited to be chair would be naive if he or she simply accepted on the basis of the invitation alone. It is important for that person to glean, as far as is possible, the following kinds of information from the administrator or other person who is doing the inviting.

Knowing Your Assignment's Limits and Demands

What are the deadlines and the time given to reach them? Most designated committees are given a discrete deadline for finishing their work, which should be more or less reasonably related to the magnitude of the committee's task. Some of these ingredients are negotiable. When I was asked by the chancellor to chair the blue-ribbon committee on intercollegiate athletics in December 1990, a deadline of June 1, 1991, was specified. I had already agreed to be away on lecture tours for a couple of 2-week periods in the spring of 1991, so I asked for the work to begin right away, for the right to designate a vice chair to chair in my absence, and for flexibility in extending the deadline for a month if necessary. All this was readily granted.

With respect to the amount of time required of you as a chair, you must expect misinformation if not lies from the person who is asking you to serve. He or she will inevitably say that you can do it with your left hand, that it will not intrude on other obligations, or something to that effect. It is in the interest of the administrator, whose main motive is to persuade, to underestimate what you will have to do. In reality, assuming the assignment of chair of a major committee means that you agree to spend whatever time is necessary. You agree to handle all unexpected contingencies that might arise during the course of the committee's work, and no one can really predict what these will be.

Knowing the Committee's Purpose

As I indicated in Chapter 2, the formal charge to the committee is normally a "high road" document, raising generic questions and leaving the answers to them open. In addition to knowing the charge, you as chair need an honest political briefing with respect to what aims the administrator has in mind and especially with respect to the organizational troubles that may lurk behind the decision to launch the committee. You should try to discern—preferably by asking directly —if the administrator has any advance preferences for recommendations, though you must also expect some caginess in the answers to such a question. You should also try to determine what constituencies are interested in the committee's problem. As prospective chair you should also receive assurances that you can return to the appointing administrator whenever necessary during the course of the committee's work in case unanticipated problems arise.

Sometimes you will find that your committee is being formed without special urgency. When I was asked to chair a special committee to review the University of California Press in 1985, the press was not in any particular trouble at the time; someone in authority had discovered, however, that it had never been reviewed formally by a faculty committee in its 93 years of existence, and suggested that it was about time. In other cases, you may not discover why a committee has been formed even if you ask. This has occurred on several occasions when I have been asked to chair an external committee for an academic department in an college or university other than my own. Assuming that the review is not simply a routine one (for example, one conducted every five years), it is safe to assume that the department is troubled in some way. About 10 years ago I recall asking the crucial "political agenda" question of an administrator who was asking me to chair such a committee. He was extremely guarded and general in answering, possibly because he did not know the whole story but probably because—as I observed earlier—administrators are often reluctant to acknowledge the depth of an institutional problem because it seems to imply administrative failure. Neither were the leaders of the department under review forthcoming; they had written up a "self-review" that was a most benign and optimistic document. Almost immediately after the committee gathered on the scene for its 2-day review, however, a few faculty members broke ranks and began to "sing" about the department's woes, and in a very short time we uncovered a most virulent and destructive situation of conflict in the department. Needless to say, the initial tight-lipped response of the parties involved in the review created a special problem for the review committee. If it was going to be at all honest in carrying out its task, it would have to write a story that it was not asked to write.

Knowing What Resources to Expect

How much information and support will be generated for the committee? In most cases a committee is not endowed and proceeds as a group of individuals who gather periodically to review a situation. Sometimes the work is sufficiently complex and important, however, that the committee is called on to bolster its work with extensive interviews or "hearings," as well as extensive documentation. In such cases you should ensure that adequate staff help is available to schedule meetings, gather information, and even draft materials.

Knowing the Committee's Size and Composition

The sensible administrator who is forming a committee should first ask you as prospective chair to serve, before approaching other members, and inform you about whom else he intends to ask. He should give you the right to veto a limited number of these—on grounds of known incompatibility with you or other suggested members' known unsatisfactory past performance—and to suggest alternatives or additions, all within the constraints of the need to represent the relevant constituencies on the committee.

Negotiating Before Accepting the Chair

Insofar as the above items permit negotiation, you are well advised to do this before accepting the chairmanship. If not, you will discover that your negotiating power is greatly reduced. It is something like the new faculty recruit who has been invited but who has not yet accepted a faculty position. That period of courtship constitutes the sole window of negotiating opportunity for the invitee—who is completely powerless before being asked and equally powerless after accepting—to make known his or her demands for salary, teaching load, and so on. Otherwise, it will be too late.

Once the committee's work has begun, you as chair will face several tasks as well as dilemmas. In facing these, I have found the following guidelines to be most helpful.

Responding Directly to the Collective Task

If a committee does its work conscientiously and expects to be effective, it must respond to the charge in a substantive, not a vapid way. As chair of any committee that I have served on, I invariably have had my own personal preferences about the issues facing the committee: the policy of the University of California Press toward publishing trade books versus monographs, for example, or the importance of revenue-producing sports such as football in athletic programs in general and on the Berkeley campus in particular. The dilemma is this: How much should you as chair push for your own predilections with respect to such issues, and how much should you push to have *some* consensus—not necessarily your own view—on the issue? Conceivably you can do both, but that is not easy, because the generally understood constraints found in the committee culture are that the chair should try to guide the committee toward consensus, not push his or her own view unduly. I have always been torn by this dilemma and have never solved it. Presumably subtlety and manipulation can carry you part way toward both gaining consensus and having your own way, but sooner or later a committee with any integrity will smell you out and resist.

Keeping the Business Moving Without Hurrying

Any committee is faced constantly with the possibility of stagnation in its progress and consequently failure in its work. This is especially true for personnel search committees. These committees face many constraints on the speed of their progress in today's atmosphere: needs to advertise the position publicly, give interested applicants ample time to apply, winnow the list and prepare a short list, schedule interviews, and so on.

Search committees are also faced with the delicate need to reach consensus on long-term commitments to persons, and that kind of consensus is often more difficult to reach than it is on many other kinds of issues. This is especially true if searches are made in politically divided academic departments that have a difficult time agreeing on anything. All these items consume a great deal of time and patience, and as a result, the greatest peril for a search committee is that it bogs down and fails to complete its task. This calls for a special kind of aggressiveness—just to keep the process moving—on your part if you are the chair of a search committee.

Other kinds of deliberative committees face the danger of stalling, too. I have already noted that a special characteristic—or perhaps disease—of academic committees is that they nearly always start with philosophical, square-one issues. Because they seem to enjoy being on that square, it is often difficult to move them from it toward a more instrumental mode. Once moved forward, moreover, committees are forever tempted to move back to square one. In addition, committees often hit a snag when one or two members put forth a position that is evidently unacceptable but will not stop pressing their position even when discouraged. Or occasionally, when the committee is nearing the end of its work, some member may unexpectedly come up with a huge area of concern—or pet recommendation—that the committee has not considered and insist that it be resolved. All these situations will turn your hair gray, because your job as chair is to move things toward a conclusion.

The corresponding dilemma for you as chair is this: How much should you remain in a permissive posture? This is important for letting everyone have a say and feeling included, but it will have you falling behind. How much should you push the committee actively ahead? This might be necessary, but it is likely to be read as "steamrollering." (This dilemma can be posed as a tug-of-war between the instrumental and expressive exigencies of committee work.)

As chair, I have found it essential to be very permissive for a substantial period of time at the early stages of a committee's work, a period that is explicitly defined as a time for exploration, not for decision. This kind of permissiveness accomplishes its stated point of allowing free inquiry without arousing the tension associated with commitment. It leaves time for people to remain at square one for a time; this is essential, because if people are forced to move away from square one prematurely, they are bound to insist on returning to it later, as to anything repressed. Equally important, somewhat leisurely exploration in the early phases permits time for posturing by individual members—which also, if repressed, will return—as well as time for people to become acquainted with one another, to sort out one another interpersonally, and to form whatever bonds they might, free from the pressure of decision making.

Sooner or later, however, it is essential to make the transition from permissiveness to decisiveness, and it usually falls to the chair to manage that process. In doing that you must devise ways both to dampen the impulses of eager committee members who are pressing for action and to move sluggish members forward. I have discovered two effective ways of accomplishing this transition:

❶ Bring the need for transition right into the open. That is, politely inform the committee that it has been enjoying the luxury of free exploration long enough, and then ask its indulgence to move ahead to more practical matters of deciding, recommending, and putting things in writing. In using this strategy, you preserve your legitimacy by asking permission to be directive.

❷ Use a kind of stick-and-carrot strategy by threatening more and longer meetings if the committee cannot get down to business or fewer and shorter meetings if it does.

This seems to work. I hope I do not appear condescending in making the following observation, but it seems to work because committee members resemble schoolchildren in that they do not like to be worked too hard and they hunger for breaks, recesses, and early dismissal from class. I know that, as a member, I respond to those kinds of threats and rewards from chairs, and I assume that members respond in the same way when I am chair.

Openness and Accommodation

I have witnessed chairs who make a point of complimenting members in one way or another on anything they might say, no matter how inane that might be. Sometimes that is effective, but I have never been able to bring myself to do it, because I am certain that I would convey an air of phoniness if I tried. Nevertheless, it is important always to be open to suggestions from any quarter—inside and outside the committee—and never reject them outright. You must adopt this posture during meetings and in hearings for constituents if these are part of the proceedings. You must also be prepared to listen to and even seek out members and constituents for private discussion of their interests and ideas if this seems necessary. This stance of openness is essential, but it is also one of the things that proves most time-consuming for the chair.

Dealing Directly With Conflict

As chair, you will necessarily encounter many tense and conflict-filled moments in the course of the committee's work. It is essential to attend to these immediately, for if they are ignored or repressed, they also will return to haunt both you and the committee. Every chair will have his or her own repertoire of strategies for dealing with tension and conflict, but I should mention three in particular.

The first is the chair's capacity—which varies greatly from chair to chair—to develop synthetic but not empty formulations that give some recognition to the two or more sides of a conflict, and to put the formulations in a way that gives something but not everything to all the disputants. This, of course, is the art of compromise, and it has to be one of the effective chair's chief assets. (It is also one of the arts that may produce the camellike look to the committee report.) The second way is to work informally with the individuals and groups who are in disagreement or conflict. Most of this work is done outside rather than inside the committee. In taking this initiative, you can ask the relevant parties how strongly they feel about their points of view, if there are alternative ways of putting the issue that might be more acceptable, or if they themselves can conceive of compromises; or you may offer a compromise on your own. As often as not, these strategies prove successful, because the vast majority of people who serve on a committee are prepared to honor its culture of civility and compromise.

Third, if all else fails, you must turn to the strategy of direct conflict resolution and call for a vote. This is surely a way of resolving a conflict, because a central feature of virtually all committee cultures is that the majority rules in case of disagreement. I have always found the vote to be an unsatisfactory means of resolution in the committee setting, however, and have always done everything I could to avoid the necessity of voting when I have been chair. When I cochaired the Committee on Basic Research in the Behavioral and Social Sciences, my cochair and I managed to get through three years of committee meetings with only one formal vote taken. In retrospect this seems quite remarkable, because the committee was large (26 members), diverse (all the behavioral and social sciences, plus some more special fields of study), and dealt with some very controversial matters (such as recommending future funding for some rather than other areas of research).

The reasons why voting in committees (except as last resort) seems unsatisfactory to me is that the minority inevitably experiences a vote as a defeat and feels disgruntled in some way. These feelings, moreover, are likely to reappear in unexpected ways on other issues at some future time. A defeat in a vote, in short, runs the risk of setting the stage for the formation of a clique—with varying degrees of cohesiveness, of course—of those have been defeated. Moreover, a vote on really decisive committee issues runs a further risk of generating a minority report, which, to me, signalizes—in all but the most severe and unavoidable cases of committee polarization—a failure on the part of the chair and the committee to have done their work properly.

Staying on Top of Terminal Tensions

As chair you should take the initiative in cultivating and expressing the tensions and emotions that inevitably appear at the last stages of the committee's work: tensions and emotions associated with the finality of making decisions, the irritability of some members who still feel that they have not gotten their way, the combination of relief and sadness that the work is through and that the committee will soon die, and, above all, the accumulation of ambivalent feelings that committee members have developed toward one another during the course of the group's work. As indicated, a dinner or party after the committee finishes its work is usually a happy way to do this. It is a kind of symbolic and ritual reassertion that the group and its culture really are continuing in existence, and that such is inevitably the occasion for reminiscing, teasing, joking, and good feelings.

In setting forth these guidelines—both for members in the last chapter and for chairs in this—I have tried to be as direct and concrete as possible, but at the same time to convey the sense that contingencies always abound and that the life course and work of any given committee is different from all other committees. In a way that fact is a blessing, because it is the similarities of all committees that make them uninteresting. It is the new people, new contingencies, and new uncertainties that make them interesting and induce one to continue in that line of work.

6 | The Committee Report

A few committees in the academic world do not produce any records. Notable examples are the external, ad hoc committees at Harvard University that meet to consider new appointments and promotions. They gather in the morning, interview members of the relevant academic department and a dean or two, and perhaps discuss the candidate among themselves. They then lunch with the president, the dean of the college, and a few of their associates. Toward the end of the lunch, the president simply goes around the room, asking each individual member of the committee what—and why—he or she thinks about the candidate. No vote is taken, no written report is presented. The president thanks the committee, and it dissolves.

At the end of the twentieth century, however, this kind of committee is something of a rarity. Almost all committees keep minutes or records of their decisions, and in many cases they submit a final product, the committee report. I consider that product in this chapter.

The Structure of the Report

For certain kinds of committees, all reports are strikingly similar in structure if not content. At the very beginning of a

---

Box 6.1

Elements of a Search Committee's Report

A search committee's report should contain the following elements:
- A brief review of the charge to the committee
- A brief description of the search itself: how the position was advertised, how many people applied, the length of the short list, how many people were interviewed, and so on
- A few paragraphs summarizing the peculiarities of the position to be filled, plus any relevant observations about the historical and current circumstances of the organization in which the candidate will serve
- A review of the criteria used in judging the candidates
- A ranking of the top candidates, with recommendations on and a fairly detailed account of the strengths and weaknesses of each
- A final recommendation
- A more-or-less stylized account—often consisting of filling out standard forms—indicating that the search process conformed to affirmative action guidelines

---

committee's first meeting, I often jest that I was on such a committee just last year and I happen to have the final report of that committee in my briefcase. Why not, I add, take 10 minutes simply to insert new names, places, and dates and submit that report? The jest usually draws laughs because it rings true. One type of committee that produces similar reports is the search committee for a person to fill a directorship, a deanship, or some other administrative position. The report, usually 8 to 10 pages long, contains, more or less and in order, the elements shown in Box 6.1. Similarly, the

---

Box 6.2

Elements of a Committee Report:
Reviewing a Department

A department review should include the following:
- A statement of the work done by the committee—documents read, people interviewed
- An account of the general features of the department—its age structure and retirement picture, its quality and national ranking if relevant, and any special transitions it might be undergoing
- A citation of the department's strengths and weaknesses (in both research and teaching) in different areas of the academic discipline
- A description of the types and quality of faculty in the department
- An assessment of the quality of the department's graduate-training program and the undergraduate curriculum, as well as the students it teaches
- A series of recommendations for the department and the dean, either woven into the text or summarized at the end, but in either case related to the facts and arguments made in the body of the report

---

reports of external committees formed to review an academic department are usually 15 to 20 pages long and contain the elements in Box 6.2. In almost all cases more than these elements are needed for the reports of search committees and external review committees, respectively. After you gain experience on several such committees, preparing their reports becomes routine.

The structure of the reports of committees arising from the perception of organizational problems or crises are less predictable and standardized in content, and for that reason they are more challenging and engaging for the committee members. The reports I wrote on the crisis in Berkeley's School of Education, on the University of California Press, on lower-division education in the University of California, and on Berkeley's intercollegiate athletics all ran to nearly 50 written pages each. They were shaped in some degree by the charges to the committees, of course, but there was room for the development of other important points; each report, moreover, required the preparation of informed and discursive arguments. In its 8 years of its existence, the Washington-based Committee on Basic Research in the Behavioral and Social Sciences produced three full books as reports—one on past developments, one on the current status and significance, and one on the future of the behavioral and social sciences.[1] That committee's work provided the greatest challenge and the most opportunity for invention.

Strategies for Writing Committee Reports

Because I have been the chair of so many of the committees on which I have served, I have also had the responsibility for drafting the whole of all the reports of those committees. In reflecting on that great range of experiences, I have developed several ideas about proper strategies to follow in executing the committee report. I review these ideas now, occasionally providing passages from reports I have written to illustrate them.

The Chair's Role in Writing the Report

About 15 years ago I served as a member on a review committee for an organized research unit—a research center—on the Berkeley campus. The charge to the committee fell somewhere between a call for a routine review and a request to suggest long-term solutions to problems relating to the research mission of the unit. The committee was not a large one, but the chair decided to break the group down into subcommittees of two members, giving each the responsibility for investigating one problematic aspect of the center and writing up that section of the report. In preparing the final report, the chair simply put together the different drafts, added a little introductory and cementing material, and submitted the report. It was an unsatisfactory report from the standpoints of consistency of argumentation, symmetry of argumentation, and style. On the basis of that and other experiences, and on the basis of personal predilection, I decided that the best strategy is for the chair either to draft the entire final report or to subject drafts prepared by others to radical rewriting in his or her won style. The rationale lying behind this strategy can be broken into two parts:

❶ Writing is a way for the chair to maintain leadership—or, if a more candid term is desired, power—in the committee setting. It is a general rule that the one who drafts first defines the terms of the discourse and—unless the draft is radically unsatisfactory—assumes power over the meaning to be imparted by that report. That is not insignificant; assigning meanings to a situation and deriving recommendations from those meanings are the main resources that committees have. As chair of a committee I invariably end a sustained discussion by volunteering to put what appears to be the consensus into a few paragraphs "for consideration by the committee at its next meeting." That language is always amended—sometimes extensively—at subsequent meetings, but as rule it takes place *within* the context established by the first draft. If someone else has undertaken a special investigation of a special area of the committee's concern to draw up a draft, I always try to gain permission from that person to redraft his or her work myself for presentation to the committee. Maintaining control over language is one of the surest ways to exercise influence and leadership in the committee setting.

❷ A single author is able to impart a continuity of style to a committee report that multiple authors cannot. If the truth be known, almost all audiences to which committee reports are typically directed —administrators, colleagues, perhaps the press—carry the expectation that committee reports are going to be heavy, dry, and unreadable. Committees should do anything they can to overcome this expectation and engage the reader. Single authorship and an attention to matters of style are principal ways of doing this.

The Importance of Analysis and Argumentation

It is commonly thought that a special-purpose committee collects facts about the situation or problem it is supposed to investigate and submits a series of recommendations in its report. Those are correct perceptions, but they leave out the need for a crucial feature that links facts and recommendations: systematic analysis and argumentation that is based on the facts and from which the recommendations are derived. This means giving background, selecting facts, linking them with plausible assertions, and presenting them in familiar and meaningful contexts. No committee report is credible or persuasive without analysis and argumentation. Several implications follow from this point.

- *Historical context should be covered.* In reviewing the troubled situation of Berkeley's School of Education in 1981, the commission felt constrained to say something about the history of universities' schools of education in the United States: their origin, their marginal status in the academic prestige hierarchy, their tendency to have moved toward becoming social-science departments rather than training centers for teachers, and so on. We documented the history of Berkeley's School of Education along the same lines. The intention of this exposition of historical context was to set the stage and assign meaning to the subsequent recommendations for changing the school.
- *The current meaning and significance of selected facts should be elucidated.* Again, in the report on the School of Education, the commission noted that the school had evolved toward a proliferation

of divisions and programs—a higher education division, an educational psychology division, a division of language and reading, and a division of instructional re-search and curriculum development, to name a few. Then we interpreted this development. We referred to the divisions as "semi-independent fiefdoms," and spelled out several negative consequences of the divisional structure: the development of parochialism of interests in the divisions, a tendency for the school to lose interest in the subject of education in general, a deterioration of governability of the school, and a certain inflexibility and unresponsiveness in the school deriving from the fact that divisions tended to reproduce themselves in proportional strength. In making these interpretations, of course, we were simultaneously asserting that cosmopolitanism, general educational concerns, governability, and flexibility were desirable in academia (and who could argue with those criteria?). In addition, we were setting the stage for and making credible our subsequent recommendation that, if the School of Education was to continue as a unit, the divisional structure should be weakened and a stronger central administration—in the form of a more powerful dean—be installed.

• *Rhetorical devices should be employed.* In my blue-ribbon committee on intercollegiate athletics, we came out with a series of conclusions and recommendations that called for greater stress on winning athletic teams at the regional (Pacific-10 Conference) and national levels. This included the major revenue sports—football and men's basketball. In the Berkeley context, which has traditionally stressed academic excellence above all, such recommendations were surely destined to be controversial and could not simply be laid on the campus community, especially the faculty. One rhetorical strategy we used in this connection was to attempt to play down the supposed contradiction between academic and athletic "cultures." We did so by beginning the report with an appropriate academic analogy: stressing the false opposition of and conflict between the cultures of the sciences and the humanities (see Box 6.3).

After orienting the reader in this way, we went on to point out that the stereotyped distinction between the "academic" and "athletic" cultures was similarly flawed, and that the two

---

Box 6.3

A Rhetorical Introduction to a Committee Report

Several decades ago, C. P. Snow, the don at Cambridge University, wrote of "two cultures" of the university—the "scientific" and the "humanistic"—which stressed different outlooks and values and were pitted against one another in ways that were ultimately damaging to the academy. Snow's formula set off the usual flurry of spilled ink, seminar dialogue, and talk in the corridors at parties. The distinction had enough truth and struck enough nerves to merit that debate. In the end, however, the dichotomy proved to be overdrawn if not stereotyped. For one thing, there are multiple outlooks and values *among* scientists and humanists—to say nothing of social scientists and others left out by Snow. For another, his dichotomy seriously downplayed the overriding *common* commitment in academia to the intellectual mission of the University in society, to standards of scholarly research, and to the goal of educating society's coming generations. As the decades passed, Snow's daunting portrait has turned out to be one of those creative oversimplications that come to fray around the edges, lose their force, and gradually become vague by virtue of their assimilation into the complexities of the real world.

---

did not contradict one another as is commonly supposed. In fact, we located a certain "special kind of link" between them for the Berkeley campus: They both could be made consistent with Berkeley's historical preoccupation with "competitive excellence," a kind of positive code phrase around Berkeley. Furthermore, we continued to return to the shortcomings of the "two cultures" view of academics and athletics throughout the report. This little confession of strategy on my part is not to argue that we convinced anybody by this rhetorical device, but only to point out how we used it.

The reader will note that the passage quoted is written clearly enough and that it employs expositional tactics that are commonly used in academic discourse: to begin with a plausible distinction, to tear down that distinction with a series of clearly ordered points, and then to proceed to a modest conclusion that is couched sufficiently in qualifications so as to appear temperate and therefore convincing. To generalize this point: It is often persuasive to write in lucid "academese language" (if that is not some sort of oxymoron).

Perhaps I can illustrate this point once more by mentioning to a kind of spoof report I composed while I was director of the University of California's Education Abroad Program (EAP) in the United Kingdom and Ireland in 1979. The report concerned our preparation for the big Thanksgiving Day dinner party for 80 exchange students that was traditionally given by directors. I began the report—addressed to the EAP director in the central Santa Barbara office—by arguing how important it was to keep carpets in the director's home from getting soiled by food spilled during the dinner. In that connection, I said it was very important to avoid serving green peas, because they had a way of rolling off plates and getting crushed into the carpets by students' shoes. Then I went on to complain at length about how inferior British plastic plates were, because any bit of moisture would wilt them and cause food to slide off them onto the carpets. Then, in a kind of academic spoof on the spoof, I wrote the following:

> Actually, working on the paper plate problem served to deepen my thinking about the issue of green peas. After analyzing the matter, I came to the conclusion that it is not entirely fair to blame the peas *as such*. To do that is to penetrate the issue only partially. In fact I would tend put the onus on the plates rather than the peas. Almost *anything* would fall off those plates. In short, when you expand your thinking beyond green peas alone, the green pea issue becomes less significant and pressing. I

thought I would pass this insight on to you for the benefit of future Directors when they plan for Thanksgiving Day dinners.

The Importance of Style

The issue of literary style is evident in the foregoing few paragraphs. I would stress that the need for forcefulness and clarity of style can scarcely be exaggerated in the preparation of the committee report. As I indicated, potential readers of a committee report are usually prepared psychologically to be put to sleep by its dullness and impenetrability. To read a lively, understandable report thus constitutes a welcome surprise. For this reason I have always devoted as much of my energy to presentation, style, and editorial polishing as I do to anything else. It helps if one possesses a clarity and forcefulness of style; it helps to have others review one's draft material from a stylistic point of view; and in some cases it might be advisable to ask someone who writes well to help in the rewriting. I can report honestly that people who have talked to me about committee reports I have written over the years have consistently mentioned their style as much as their content.

If a report is of sufficient general interest to be picked up by the press, you should be alert to the issue of quotability. Of course, one cannot control what will be quoted from a report one writes. But it is a certainty that reporters will not quote long-winded and dry paragraphs as they present the message of the report. Clear and concise sentences on important topics are the ones likely to get picked up. Two instances come to mind, both from the report of the task force on lower-division education in the University of California:

- Early in the report we turned to the problem of the difficulty of access to overcrowded courses on many campuses of the university. At one point, in the middle of a paragraph, I wrote the following sentence: "Each term [i.e., semester or quarter] is a scramble, with students struggling to get into courses they want or need." I could not really have predicted it, but that sentence proved to be one of the most quoted in the report. The reasons for that, I believe, were both substantive (it touched the sensitivities of many parents and students) and stylistic (because the wording seemed to have a certain vividness about it).

• Very early in the report it seemed important to communicate that the task force was committed to the proposition that lower-division education was an essential element in the University of California's mission, but that there were serious problems associated with it in practice. At the same time we did not want simply to mouth the boilerplate stereotypes about undergraduate education that were the stock-in-trade of uninformed critics. After asserting the importance of collegiate education in the first two years, I chose the following wording: "Despite this role, the lower division is something of a neglected child in terms of information gathered, attention paid, and critical review given to it." This wording identified a problem but stopped short of proclaiming a situation of hopelessness. What seemed to strike readers of the report—and, even more, newspaper and magazine reporters—was the phrase "neglected child." That phrase appeared in almost every published account of the report. I suppose that it communicated that we, the faculty issuing the report, were not uncritical; but, in addition, the analogy to the family struck a chord of concern that could easily be appreciated by all readers. (Readers of this book may have noticed that I used the same ploy in the Preface when I compared the committee to a spouse in a neurotic marriage. I might add, however, that I do not expect that analogy to make it in the daily press.)

Occasionally, however, the search for just the right "mot" can backfire. In the report on the Berkeley School of Education we made a point of assigning the responsibility for the troubled state of the school to many causes. Among these was the Berkeley administration itself, which we felt had neglected the school over the years. In this connection, we described a past search for a dean that had been organized by the provost of the professional schools as "prolonged and languid," and we described the posture of the provost himself as one of "punitive starvation" toward the school. While those phrases earned me several rewarding comments from readers about their wittiness, they almost ended my long friendship with the provost himself, who did not appreciate the humorous exaggeration or perhaps appreciated it too well.

Since that episode, I have made it a point of undertaking a last-minute scan over every draft report I prepare—with one question in mind: Are there passages that seem to constitute a gratuitous slap at any party that might be interested in the report? If so, can the wording be changed to eliminate or soften the slap without losing the point? It is clear that any report with any substance is going to offend some people for some reasons in any event; the object of this kind of penultimate review is to make certain that as few as possible of such offenses are necessary.

Presenting the Recommendations

The heart of any committee report is, of course, the recommendations themselves, even though these may be greatly strengthened or weakened according to the quality of the facts, analysis, argumentation, and style in the context of which they are presented. The reason for the central importance of recommendations, moreover, is that they call for decisions to be made and resources to be allocated (and, most likely, enemies to be created). The most important points to be made about the recommendations in the final report are the following:

- Avoid a minority report. A minority report usually exacts a tax on the credibility and influence of a committee. For that reason it is important for the chair to head off such a statement if he or she can. There is one exception to this rule. Even if a committee is hopelessly divided on fundamental points, the efforts of an effective chair, combined with those of other peacemakers on the committee, can probably succeed in avoiding a minority report. At a certain point, however, that effort may result in a consensus report that is so camellike and so honeycombed with hedging and qualifications that it loses force. The larger truth involved is that any deeply divided committee can seldom write a successful report, whether that report arrives in apparently consensual form or with both majority and minority versions.

- Limit the recommendations in number and scope. I have seen reports with as many as 50 or 60 recommendations. The sheer weight of that number exhausts the audience and loses force. In the Task Force on Lower-Division Education, we consciously decided that we should have no more than a dozen recommendations, and we finally ended up with 13. We believed it important to set this limit, even though it meant ignoring many points in our charge. Furthermore, as chair and drafter, I made every effort to compress the language of every one of these recommendations so that no one would take more than several lines of text. Here are a couple of examples of recommendations in that report:

    1. Campuses should institute and expand freshman-sophomore seminars or functionally equivalent educational processes that constitute a chance for lower-division students to interact with ladder-rank faculty in a small classroom setting.

    2. Campuses should review and improve mechanisms for training, supervision, and evaluation of teaching assistants, especially at the departmental level.

    The reason for brevity and directness in making recommendations is that even knowledgeable and interested readers grow weary of vague, wordy calls for action that are couched in tiresome reservations and qualifications.

- Make the recommendations realistic, feasible, and implementable. In the lower-division task force we stated explicitly that we aimed "to observe the limits of budgetary and institutional realities in generating recommendations." We tried to do this in all cases and took note of those that required new resources. On one occasion I chaired a committee that submitted a recommendation that proved to be clearly fanciful, even though it possessed a certain analytic soundness. This was the commission on the School of Education at Berkeley. After a long and complicated analysis of many aspects of the school's situation, the commission developed some 15 separate options for reform of the school. Then, one by one, we rejected virtually all of these options. In the end we came perilously close to recommending that the Berkeley campus discontinue the school. I say "perilously close" because we hedged so much on that deadly recommendation that it became truly camel-like in shape.

A couple of days before we submitted the report to the chancellor of the campus, we met with him for an hour to outline its contents. When we told him about the "discontinuation" option, his face grew ashen. It was immediately apparent to him—and to us when we observed his expression—that such a recommendation was unrealistic. How could the California legislature—much less its alumni and other political constituents—possibly permit the elimination of the only University of California School of Education in the northern part of the state? We left the recommendation in the report anyway and submitted it. It raised great cheers among some, great cries of anguish among others, and great interest among all. But the chancellor did not follow it. Instead he picked up another of our options—one we felt was not going to be especially effective —and initiated a search for a new dean of the school, who would take an aggressive role in rebuilding it.

- For long and important reports, it is essential to have an executive summary. This is clearly not necessary for many search committee reports and reports that review departments, because they are usually of limited length and will be read in toto by the few interested parties: the department chair and his colleagues, a senate committee, the dean, and the provost.

That does not apply to longer, more complex documents. It was once said of President Eisenhower that he did not want to read anything that could not be put on a 3 × 5-in. index card. I have also heard it said of a top executive that if you wanted him or her to read something, it had better be on the first page of the report. Whether those unkind assertions are true or not, it is correct to say that almost nobody reads a 50-page report. It is only the narcissism of involved committee members who have put so much time and energy into preparation that leads them to believe that more than a handful of readers will hang on its every word. Most of those who are interested will read a crisp, two- or three-page executive summary that conveys the meat of the analysis and recommendations, permits a reasonable grasp of the report's intent, and guides them to parts of the report in which they are especially interested.

Submitting the Report

The final submission of a committee report to the cognizant dean, provost, chancellor, or parent committee is invariably an anticlimactic act. The report is usually on the anonymous side, because it is formally multiauthored, although occasionally it comes to be named after its chair. After the report is submitted, the committee is typically discharged, never to convene again.

In most cases the committee has no say in the dissemination of a report. At one extreme is the confidential report of a search committee or an ad hoc personnel committee, which is seen only by a few eyes and, it is hoped, not others. At the other extreme is the committee report that is awaited with wide interest and is simply released by the administrator to whom the committee reports. In that case, too, the committee has no influence over who will read the report or what they will make of it.

The main exception to these two extreme cases is the report written by an external review committee about an academic department. Typically this committee is appointed by a dean, to whom it is asked to give its report. It is his or her decision to show, summarize, or keep that report hidden from the department chair and faculty members. At the same time, during and after the course of the committees's review, faculty members and perhaps graduate students in the department being reviewed ask the external committee's members if and when they will see the report. The chair usually responds by saying that it is up to the dean. But it is important for the external committee members to know how wide the ultimate readership will be. They will write a different kind of report to the dean alone than they will if they know that all of their colleagues in the reviewed department will read it. My own predilection is to ask the dean to show the report to the members of the department being reviewed. Part of the reason for this is that one must assume that the contents of the report will leak out anyway, sooner or later. But in addition, I believe it both possible and important for a review committee with integrity to communicate honestly and directly with those colleagues they have reviewed. For that reason, the distribution of the full report to the interested parties is the best policy.

Beyond that exception, however, the committee loses control of its report at the moment it is submitted. It cannot recall it for reconsideration. The report may be circulated widely or it may consigned to a shelf to gather the proverbial dust. It may have as much as a great impact or as little as none. The members of the committee, or at least its chair, are usually thanked for their service by a warm but stylized note from the administrator to whom the report is submitted, and it is possible to write down that one has served on that committee when one submits an annual report to his or her department chair. Beyond that there are few rewards other than the intangible psychological gratifications that one has gained from participating. Under those circumstances, the best thing for a discharged committee to do is to have its final party and call it a day.

Note

1. See Robert McC. Adams, Neil J. Smelser, and Donald J. Treiman (Eds.), *Behavioral and Social Science Research: A National Resource* (Washington, DC: National Academy Press, 1982); Neil J. Smelser and Dean R. Gerstein (Eds.), *Behavioral and Social Science: Fifty Years of Discovery* (Washington, DC: National Academy Press, 1986); and Dean R. Gerstein, R. Duncan Luce, Neil J. Smelser, and Sonja Sperlich, *The Behavioral and Social Sciences: Achievements and Opportunities* (Washington, DC: National Academy Press, 1988).

7 | Committees and Careers

After having invested a significant portion of my own career in committee work, and after having invested thought, energy, and time in writing this book, I suppose I have reasons—mainly those of self-justification—for pushing committee work and arguing that it is a major part of an academic career. So it is important for me to allow straight out that it is not *the* or even *a* major ingredient. Work on committees does count, however, and I devote these last few pages to putting that work in the context of an academic career.

If committee service is transparently not at center stage in your career, how does it fit in? There are at least three reasons why it is important:

❶ *Rewards.* In the personnel manual of the University of California, the language is that academic advancement should be based on four criteria: scholarship, creative activity (read "publication" for this), university service, and service to the profession and community. The list is much the same for all major research institutions. As one moves toward state universities and liberal arts colleges, the stress on teaching increases and that on publication decreases, but in those institutions the latter now enters more into the career of academics than it did several decades ago. In community colleges the stress is almost exclusively on teaching and service.

Committee work is found under the categories of service to the university and service to the profession and community. As a rule, these two kinds of activity do not count very heavily in the minds of deans and personnel committees. Even if your performance is stellar in these areas, you are not likely to be rewarded by merit increases or promotions, especially if your research is poor or nonexistent and your teaching is mediocre or bad. But if you are completely inactive with respect to service, this will catch up with you and your career, especially if, in the long haul, you earn the unenviable rap that you do not pull your oar. It is oversimple to say that effective committee work cannot help your career much but its absence can hurt it, but this statement is not too far off the mark.

❷ *Citizenship*. Earlier I mentioned that the idea of a calling—of which collective commitment to the enterprise is a part—is still alive in the academic world, even though it has weakened. Part of that calling is service to the college or university, and part of that service is a reasonable amount of committee work. It comes with the territory. It is part of the largely implicit bargain that you, as an academic, strike with your institution: You are awarded security of career—of which tenure is the concrete form—as well as great flexibility and minimal day-by-day supervision. A part of the other side of that bargain includes the notion of service, that you will give some of your time—almost always unpaid—to the collective purposes of the institution. That constitutes a reason for participating in committee work.

❸ *Quality of life*. There is a positive and a negative aspect to this heading. Committee work outside the department—that is, for the college or university as a whole and for the profession and the community—is a way of diversifying your existence, breaking out from departmental boundaries, and meeting others unlike yourself and your colleagues. It is, in short, a way of enriching your professional experience. On the negative side, shunning committee work altogether or performing irresponsibly in it earns you the disdain of those colleagues who *do* pull their oars and in that and other ways makes for a kind of professional isolation.

If we extrapolate from this reasoning, we can envision three possible career approaches to working on committees. First, you may avoid it altogether. As I have indicated, it is not mandatory for you to participate in committee life, even though failing to do so may have some long-term and indirect negative effects on your career. But if you know yourself to be inept or if you have an unbounded distaste for committee work, you can avoid it by consistently saying no. Sooner or later, moreover, you will not have to say no, because you will cease being asked because you have developed a reputation of being a nonserver. If you do not mind risking the minor career disadvantages, and if you do not mind the isolation and lack of collective involvement, then consistent refusal is one real option.

Second, and at the other extreme, is the committee "junkie," who makes committee service a way of life, compulsively seeking out and serving on every possible committee. There are an identifiable number of old committee hands of this sort on every campus. While they often serve the institution well in this capacity, committee "junkies" are frequently the target of ambivalence on the part of their colleagues, because "junkiness" implies that they have become addicted and are thus shortchanging their other professional obligations of research and teaching. You must be on guard against overserving, especially if you find committee work enjoyable. The temptations are there: The more effectively you serve, the more often you will be asked to serve again, because administrators and others appreciate your contributions and profit from your free labor.

The third career line is intermediate between the two extremes, and, not surprisingly, is the one I recommend. It is the golden mean once again, the role of making responsible and effective committee work a part of your career, but not letting it get out of hand. To safeguard against the latter, it necessary to maintain two kinds of balance:

❶ *Balance between committee work and other career considerations.* Part of this is keeping in perspective exactly how important (an unimportant) committee work is for your whole career. In this connection, you should be wary of illusions about committee work, especially writing projects, by taking on yet another committee assignment: The illusion that you will be rewarded more than you will, the illusion that your services are indispensable and that no one else can do the job, the illusion that you are near or at the center of power when you serve on committees, and the illusion that it does not matter if you postpone the realization of other projects. Furthermore, if you are a moderately successful and responsible academic, it is no crime to say no to a request to serve on a committee, especially if you already have a good record and if you cite other, compelling career demands on your time.

❷ *Balance among different kinds of committee work.* If you have the view that committee work is necessary but that all committee work is alike—that is, equally distasteful—then you will tend to serve on one committee or another without discriminating between them. In most cases this approach is a mistaken one. Some types of committee work fit your career intentions and interests more than others, and you should make an effort, largely through self-examination, to determine what these are and do your service in ways that are interesting and important to you. This means saying yes to some requests and no to others. Furthermore, work on committees is often negotiable. For instance, if your department chair asks you to undertake a particularly distasteful committee assignment, as often as not you can get out of it by volunteering for another, more agreeable one. Because your chair usually needs your service more than you need to serve, such negotiation has a good chance of yielding the outcome you want. The negotiating strategy, moreover, is usually more comfortable in the long run than simply saying no all the time.

It follows from all this that one of the most important things you must know about committee service is your own mind. Is a request to serve reasonable according to your own tastes? What will you get out of it, both in terms of current gratification and future possibilities? Will it be exciting or boring? Does the prospect of committee work, as defined, promise to contribute to an aspect of organizational life you value? Or, alternatively, do you have political, moral, or other personal reasons to object to the purposes of the committee? On the basis of your answers to such questions you will decide to serve or not to serve. If you decide to serve but then decide—

on one ground or another—that you have made a mistake, it is essential to resign early and give forthright reasons for resigning. If you do not resign and decide to tough it out, you risk many possibilities, almost all negative: You will be bored, you will be alienated, you will compromise your convictions, you will generate bad blood among your committee colleagues because you are not cooperative, or you will look like one or another sort of fool.

If, after consulting your own mind, you decide to serve on a committee, it seems the wisest policy to try to make your work effective rather than ineffective. If the latter, you end up wasting everybody's time, especially your own. Throughout this book—especially in Chapters 4 and 5—I have attempted to lay out the organizational context of committee work and the nature of the dynamics of committees. Within those contexts I have tried to generate the most sensible and practical rules of thumb about committee work, acknowledging at the same time that they cannot be regarded as mechanical maxims that apply always and everywhere. With that final word, our meeting is adjourned.

Appendix

What follows is a list of committees—more or less in chronological order—on which I have served since my appointment as an Assistant Professor on the Berkeley campus of the University of California in the fall of 1958. Not all of these committees are mentioned in the text of the book, but reflections based on the experience accumulated from all of them are represented there.

Member, Chancellor's Committee on Discrimination, Berkeley campus, 1960-1961. Investigated issues and situations relating to racial and ethnic discrimination on the Berkeley campus.

Member, Committee on Economic Growth, Social Science Research Council, New York, 1961-1965. Planned and organized conferences and publications, awarded small research grants.

Member, Executive Committee of the American Sociological Association, 1962-1965. Interim governing committee of the ASA between council meetings.

Member, Publications Committee of the American Sociological Association, 1962-1965. Made policy decisions and editorial appointments relating to the publications of the ASA.

Member, various informal faculty "campus crisis" committees during the free speech movement on the Berkeley campus, 1964.

Member, Committee on Pieces of Paper, Chancellor's Office, Berkeley campus, 1965. Read and made recommendations concerning written communications issued by various campus offices and agencies to Berkeley faculty and students.

Member, Board of Educational Development, Berkeley campus, 1966-1968. Reviewed projects for educational experiments and innovations submitted by Berkeley faculty and students; recommended support and funding.

Chair, Sociology Panel of the Behavioral and Social Sciences Survey, sponsored by the Social Science Research Council and the National Academy of Sciences, 1967-1969. Prepared a volume on the current state of sociology as a discipline and made recommendations concerning research and institutional support and foundations.

Member, Task Group on Research and Development in Education, President's Science Advisory Committee, 1968. Made recommendations on funding of research and development in education by the federal government.

Member, Technical Advisory Committee, Carnegie Commission on Higher Education, 1968-1973. Advised Clark Kerr, chair of the commission, on policies and projects relating to higher education.

Member, Policy Committee of the Berkeley Academic Senate, 1970-1971, Chair, 1971-1972. Generated policies in the academic senate and consulted with the chancellor of the Berkeley campus.

Member, Committee on Problems and Policy, Social Science Research Council, 1975-1977. Made policies relating to the research support activities of the council.

Member, Steering Committee of the Undergraduate Curriculum Development Group of the American Political Science Association, 1975-1977. Recommended curricular changes in undergraduate programs in political science.

Member, Advisory Committee, Carnegie Council on Higher Education Project on the Undergraduate Curriculum, 1976-1977, 1979-1980.

Member, Nominations Committee, Social Science Research Council, 1979-1980. Made nominations for the SSRC.

Chair, Educational Policy Committee of the Academic Senate, University of California, Berkeley, and Member, Universitywide Educational Policy Committee, 1979-1980. Reviewed matters of educational policy on the Berkeley campus.

Member, Special Projects Committee, Center for Advanced Study in the Behavioral Sciences, 1979-1992; chair, 1984-1992. Made recommendations for special research project groups at the Center.

Cochair, Research Committee on Economy and Society, International Sociological Association, 1980-1986. Organized research projects, conferences, and programs at the world congresses of the ISA.

Member, Committee on Basic Research in the Behavioral Sciences, Assembly of the Behavioral and Social Sciences, National Research Council and National Academy of Sciences, 1980-1988; chair, 1982-1984; cochair, 1984-1988. Developed several national reports on basic research in the behavioral and social sciences.

Chair, Commission to Review the School of Education, University of California, Berkeley, 1981. Reviewed and made recommendation on the reorganization of the school.

Member, Committee on Nominations, American Academy of Arts and Sciences, 1981-1984. Nominated officers for the academy.

Chair, External Advisory Committee for Sociology, Harvard University, 1981-1986. Advised the president and dean of the college on the status of and personnel appointments in the Department of Sociology at Harvard.

Member, Subcommittee on Humanism, American Board of Internal Medicine, American Medical Association, 1981-1984, 1989-1990. Recommended evaluation measures and assessment of humanistic traits in residents in training in internal medicine.

Chair, Committee to Review the University of California Press, 1984-1985. Prepared a report on the policies and operations of the University of California Press.

Chair, Task Force on Lower-Division Education in the University of California, 1985-1986. Reviewed and prepared recommendations on undergraduate education in the freshmen and sophomore years for the university president's office.

Member, Executive Committee, International Sociological Association, 1986-1990, 1990-1994. Governs the association between council meetings at the world congresses of the ISA.

Member, Program Committee, International Sociological Association, 1986-1994; Chair, 1990-1994. Plans and organizes programs for the world congresses of the ISA.

Member, President's Advisory Committee on Undergraduate Education, University of California, 1987-1989. Advised the president's office of the university on policies and programs related to undergraduate education.

Member, Yale Council Committee to Review the Social Sciences (Behavioral) at Yale University, 1988-1993. Reviews and advises the university president on the departments of anthropology, psychology, and sociology.

Member, Committee on Committees, Berkeley Division of the Academic Senate, 1988-1989. Appointed members to all academic senate committees and advised the Berkeley administration on the composition of administrative committees on the campus.

Member, Scientific and Academic Advisory Committee to the President of the University of California on the Energy Laboratories (Livermore and Los Alamos), 1988-1993. Oversight committee for the weapons laboratory of the federal Department of Energy.

Member, Audits Committee, Russell Sage Foundation Board of Trustees, 1990-1991. Reviewed audit statements of the foundation.

Member, Nominations Committee, Russell Sage Foundation Board of Trustees, 1992-1993. Seeks and nominates new members to the board.

Member, Advisory Committee to the Board, American Board of Internal Medicine, 1992-1995. Reviews policy matters for the board and reports to it.

Member of approximately eight search committees for directors and other academic administrative officers, 1960-present.

Member of approximately 25 departmental committees of the Department of Sociology, University of California Berkeley, 1960-present. Committees included admissions, graduate evaluation, personnel, graduate and undergraduate curriculum. Chaired many of these.

Member of approximately 15 ad hoc personnel review committees, University of California, Berkeley, 1960-present.

Member of approximately 12 external review committees of sociology departments outside my own university. Chaired all but three.

In addition to this committee work, I have served in a variety of other capacities that were not committees in the strict sense of the word but which functioned much as committees do. These positions are the following:

Member, Board of Directors, Social Science Research Council, 1969-1973; Chair of the Board, 1971-1973.

Chair, Department of Sociology, University of California, Berkeley, 1974-1976, 1991-1992.

Member, Board of Trustees, Center for Advanced Study in the Behavioral Sciences, 1981-1993; Chair of the Board, 1986-1988.

Chair, Berkeley Division of the Academic Senate of the University of California, 1982-1984.

Vice Chair and Chair, Academic Council and Academic Assembly of the Academic Senate, University of California, 1985-1987. This was the universitywide academic senate.

Faculty Representative to the Board of Regents of the University of California, 1985-1987. Sat as nonvoting member of the board.

Member, Board of Trustees, Russell Sage Foundation, 1990-1995.

About the Author

Neil J. Smelser (Ph.D., Harvard University, 1958) has served on the sociology faculty of the University of California, Berkeley, for 35 years. He currently holds the title University Professor of Sociology. He is the author of many books, including *Theory of Collective Behavior* (1962), *Comparative Methods in the Social Sciences* (1976), and *Social Paralysis and Social Change* (1991). He also edited *Handbook of Sociology* (1988). He has been elected as a member of the American Academy of Arts and Sciences, and the National Academy of Sciences, the American Philosophical Association, and is now Vice President of the American Sociological Association.